# La Conquistadora

Fray Angelico Chavez

# LA CONQUISTADORA
The Autobiography of an Ancient Statue

Sunstone Press
Santa Fe, New Mexico

Cover art by Kris Hotvedt

Sunstone books may be purchased for educational, business, or sales promotional use. For
information please write: Special Markets Department, Sunstone Press, P.O. Box 2321, Santa Fe,
New Mexico 87504-2321.

REVISED EDITION

10 9 8 7 6 5 4 3 2

Library of Congress Cataloging-in-Publication Data:
Chavez, Angelico, 1910–
    La Conquistadora.

    Bibliography

    1. Conquistadora (Statue) 2. Cathedral of San Francisco de Asis (Santa Fe, N.M.)–
History. 3. Catholic Church–New Mexico–Santa Fe–History. 4. Santa Fe (New Mexico)–
Church history.
I. Title.
BT660.S45C5     1975     282'.78956     81-14473
ISBN: 0-913270-43-1                 AACR2

Published by    SUNSTONE PRESS
                Post Office Box 2321
                Santa Fe, NM 87504-2321 / USA
                (505) 988-4418 / orders only (800) 243-5644
                FAX (505) 988-1025
                www.sunstonepress.com

# TO THE MEMORY

## Of These and Scores of Other "Conquistadora" Progenitors and Their Consorts

———

ANA ROBLEDO and FRANCISCO GÓMEZ
who begat

Andrés Gómez Robledo
who begat

Francisca Gómez Robledo
who bore

| | |
|---|---|
| Maria Roybal<br>who bore | Matéo Roybal<br>who begat |
| Juliana Archevéque<br>who bore | |
| Miguel Gabaldón<br>who begat | Mariano Roybal<br>who begat |
| Juana Gabaldón<br>who bore | Juan Manuel Roybal<br>who begat |
| Toribio Luna<br>who begat | |
| Encarnación Luna<br>who bore | Desiderio Roybal<br>who begat |
| Eugenio Chávez<br>who begat | Romualdo Roybal<br>who begat |
| Fabián Chávez | Nicolasa Roybal |

who are the parents of

THE AUTHOR

FORMA ORIGINALIS
...V. M. de S<sup>mo</sup> ROSARIO
...A CONQUISTADORA
...INA ANTIQUI REGNI
...NOVI-MEXICI...

RESTAURATIO EX ...
...CIIS IN IPSA IMAG...
IN ASSUMPTIONE ...
A GUSTAVO BAUMANN
... FR. ANGELICO, O.F.M.

# TABLE OF CONTENTS

# PROLOGUE

I AM A *small wooden statue of the Blessed Virgin Mary, dressed in real clothes of silk and gold braid like a Spanish Queen of old, and I have been in this country for more than three hundred and twenty-five years. Every single year of that long span I have been taken out in procession, and not a day has passed without someone breathing a tender prayer to the Mother of God in my presence. This not only makes me the oldest representation of Mary in this nation, but also one which has continually received daily homage as an unworthy proxy of heaven's Queen. Since the day I came, I have never been consigned to an attic or a storeroom; I have always been in the midst of my people, in their joys as well as in their sorrows — yes, even in battle.*

*My name for centuries has been "La Conquistadora." This is because I came to the Southwest with the Spanish pioneers who called themselves conquistadores. It is really a popular nickname, given to me by a people who regarded me with loving intimacy, like folks in more recent times who affectionately called a famous dancer "La Argentina." Such endearing terms cannot be put into English without losing their color and flavor. "The Lady Conqueror," for example, is quite literal, but much too cold. The most correct rendering is "Our Lady of the Conquest," but, while it carries all the color of Spanish arms, it does not convey the warmth of Spanish hearts. So you might as well call me, as you would spell it, "La Con-kees-tah-do-rah."*

*Nor do I mind being compared with actresses, for, like one, I have played the part of Mary in different glorious roles. In the beginning I was "Our Lady of the Assumption," then for a short time "The Immaculate Conception," and finally "Our Lady of the Rosary." In these titles I was regarded by my people as Queen of New Mexico and of Santa Fe, but all the while, as with a beloved actress, I have been popularly known as La Conquistadora.*

*As I said at the start, I have been in this country for more than three centuries and a quarter, but I am much older. Exactly how old, only the Lord and I know, and a lady, even a wooden one, will not tell her exact age. All I can say is that long, long ago, there was a big willow tree in a faraway land. On the meadow all around it bloomed flowers of every color and shade, and the willow wept because it was always green, while the meadow wore dresses of every hue as the seasons varied. Then one day a man came and chopped the tree to the ground. Both the bole and the branches were to be cut into smaller parts, and these split into smaller pieces, and all would be burned to ashes in somebody's hearth. This was the end, the willow knew, and it was just as well; for this was the usual fate of trees.*

*Every bit of the willow went into the fire when the pieces had dried out, all except one. And this was because another man picked up a small section of trunk and took it home, to his little shop filled with chisels and mallets and unfinished statues. From the moment he saw it, the woodcarver liked this piece of wood for being so light and firm, as well as flawless and easy to carve. Then one day I was no longer a short willow log, but a beautiful woman standing on a graceful pedestal. Beneath my feet was a cloud from which peered the chubby faces of three happy cherubs.*

*My long gown showed only at the hem in front and for a short space above my left foot, and at the narrow sleeves of my entire right arm and up to the elbow of my left arm. The rest was covered by an Oriental scarf wrapped across my breast, and by a large gracefully folded mantle that dropped lightly from my head down to my feet. One edge of this large*

9

*veil fell over my left ear onto my left shoulder and breast, and was caught in folds under my bent forearm. The other edge fell behind my right ear to cover my entire back, and then was brought over my right thigh and slightly bent knee to be tucked with the other folded edge beneath my left arm.*

*All the garments were first covered with a velvet-smooth plaster, which was painted crimson and then covered with gold leaf. On this golden surface were traced tiny scrolled and ribbed designs, arabesques, in red, orange, and blue. It was a unique dress, not the classic gown and mantle usually seen on pictures and statues of the Virgin, but rather the costume of Moorish princesses who once brightened the halls and courts of the Alhambra — truly, the dress also of a Lady of Palestine.*

*My two slender hands were held folded before my breast. My light brown tresses showed slightly above my clear brow and again revealed themselves at the sides of my neck underneath the ears. With my head raised a little, faintly smiling, I gazed heavenward in expectation. On seeing me complete for the first time, the good sculptor's wife recognized me right away and exclaimed:*

*"How beautiful! How precious! It is the Assumption of holy Mary into heaven!"*

* * *

*I remember, later on, a journey over water — an ocean, or a lake, it does not matter. Next I found myself in a different land, for most of the people were very dark, but with pleasing features. They liked me very much, as I gathered from their gaze and from their remarks made in Spanish or in their own tongues. This was the city of Mexico, capital of a country in the New World which was then known as New Spain. And it was here that Father Alonso first saw me and loved me.*

# CHAPTER I

FRAY Alonso de Benavides was a middle-aged Franciscan in the great city of Mexico who had been appointed to preside over the missions in the mysterious new kingdom of New Mexico, far in the fabulous northland. A native of the Azores, he had been a bailiff for the Holy Office as a layman, but shortly after coming to the New World he entered the Franciscan Order and was later ordained a priest. A man of untiring vigor, he had not only served as the superior of various friaries and as master of novices, but had also worked for the Holy Office in many important assignments, up to the year 1623, when he was ordered to New Mexico. There he would rule the Church not only as head of the missions but also as the delegate of the Holy Office. A less glamorous task in the beginning was to gather all kinds of supplies for his new missions, which he was informed were in desperate need, and to arrange for their transportation.

It was then that he first saw me and called me beautiful with his eyes. His heart decided at once that I would go with him to Santa Fe, and there reign in its parish church of the Assumption. Not only did my loveliness captivate Father Alonso, but my small self was just right, since it was impractical to haul large statues, in those early days, on a journey by oxcart that took at least three months over trackless mountains and deserts. And a man like Father Alonso had little trouble in getting my owner to part with me.

We left the city of Mexico early in the year 1625, when

the oxcart train of every three years departed for the kingdom and missions of New Mexico. I was carefully enclosed in a strong case forty inches long, twenty-four inches wide, and twenty-two deep; this case was then nailed inside a sturdy wooden box. I rode on top of other crates in a lumbering cart, one of a string of such *carretas* rolling on two massive wooden wheels, and drawn by teams of heavy oxen. Around us on horseback rode a new governor on his way to Santa Fe, Don Felipe Sotelo, with his retinue of aides, while his servants went on foot or on burros. Also on horseback was an escort of soldiers from New Mexico under their commander, Captain Francisco Gómez. Father Alonso and several new missionaries going with him were mounted on mules.

At the north end of the vast Valley of Mexico, we paused by a rocky hill, called Tepeyac. After taking a good view of the valley, dotted by the white city among bright shimmering lakes, and small white towns in every direction, all, from the ox drivers and servants to the governor and the friars, went over to an imposing church at the foot of the hill. Its delicately carved stone entrance and towers shone white and new in the morning sun; for it had been finished only three years before, in 1622, replacing a former structure of ninety years. My companions went in to say farewell to Our Lady of Guadalupe and to ask her for a safe journey.

Most of you already know about the heavenly painting of Our Lady of Guadalupe. It could be that someone might suspect that I, as a woman, could be jealous of a rival representation of the Mother of God. I am only jesting, of course. But because I want to tell her story myself, and also because so much of what happened here comes into my adventures in various ways, I shall relate the wonders of Mexico's Guadalupe as my oxcart creaks and bounces on its slow plodding way northward to Santa Fe. *Ave Maria Puríssima.*

In the year 1531, ninety-four years before this my departure from the city of Mexico, there lived a very humble and simple Indian, fifty-five years old, in the hill country north of Tepeyac — and here blessed Mary appeared to him.

Juan Diego — these were his Spanish name and surname recently received in baptism — was on his way to the friars' church of St. James in the suburb of Tlatelolco, to attend the weekly Mass of the Virgin, on Saturday, the ninth of December. It was only ten years and some four months since Hernán Cortés had conquered the city of Mexico and the surrounding country, but already the valley had several churches. The city was already a bishopric, and the first bishop-elect, the holy Fray Juan de Zumárraga, had built his first cathedral in honor of the Immaculate Conception on the very spot where the Aztecs had not long ago offered human sacrifices to the Plumed Serpent. Thousands and thousands of Indians had been converted, yet oldish Juan Diego had but recently been baptized. Whatever the reason, he made up for this delay by being a very good neophyte.

On this early morning of the ninth of December, as I was just saying, Juan Diego was trotting down the path that skirted one side of Tepeyac, at daybreak, anxious not to miss the Saturday Mass in honor of Mary, when he heard beautiful sounds floating down from the hilltop, like the warbling of innumerable birds. He stopped short and, looking up, saw a glowing white cloud that shone with a blinding light in its center. This radiance, in turn, haloed the cloud with a rainbow of many hues. Never had Juan Diego seen such a dawn. Fixed in his tracks with wonderment, he heard a sweet voice calling him by name and bidding him to come close, which he did in the same unbroken rapture. In the middle of the radiant cloud which, by the way, seemed to turn the rocks all about into many-colored precious stones, he saw a Beautiful Maiden smiling at him.

She addressed him most sweetly: "Juan Diego, my child, whom I so dearly love for being so little and guileless, where are you going?"

Quite at ease in her presence, like a trusting child, he answered simply that he was on his way to hear Mass, without even bothering to ask who she was and what she was doing on that lonely rocky hilltop at such an hour. However, she supplied for his simplicity.

"I want you to know, my dear child, that I am the ever-Virgin Mary, Mother of the true God, Author of life, Creator of all things, and Lord of heaven and earth, who is everywhere . . ."

These phrases he understood, for they had been drilled into him by the friar-catechists to drive out former notions regarding many gods that could do only certain things and held sway in only certain places. And now she further charged him to go into the center of the city where the bishop lived, and to tell him that she wanted a chapel built here. For here she would display her tender mercies in behalf of all of Juan Diego's people. The Indian readily promised to go, having understood her thoroughly because she spoke in the Nahuatl or Aztec tongue, the only language that he knew.

The bishop's household servants and secretaries were less than impressed by this uncouth Indian from the hills who claimed to have an urgent message for his lordship. But when the latter was finally told that there was a common old Indian who would not leave his doorstep until he delivered a secret message in person, Juan Diego was ushered in at once. Fray Juan de Zumárraga, who was a true son of St. Francis, listened with kind attention, as though Juan Diego were his equal. However, as an educated man, he knew that good lowly folks, and sometimes even he himself, might easily imagine things. As a judge of the Holy Office in Spain, he had examined people accused of sorcery, and had found them to be poor, harmless, deluded creatures. Juan Diego could be one of these, and so he dismissed him with many thanks and much kindness.

That evening, just after sundown, Juan Diego was on his way home when he saw the Lady again on the crest of Tepeyac. "My very dear child," he now addressed her; but he added, as if to correct himself, "my Queen and Most High Lady." Then he related his adventures at the bishop's house, begging her to send someone else, some noble and highborn person who would be believed more readily. The Lady, however, replied that she had no dearth of servants and messengers, but that she wanted him and none other to deliver her message. Juan Diego quickly answered that the trip and the hardships about seeing the bishop were no trouble at all; he was only taking his own lowly self into account. Of course he would do it all over again. Then he trudged on home.

Early next day, the tenth of December, Juan Diego went to Sunday Mass at Tlatelolco, and stayed for catechism. From there he went to see the bishop, only to go through the same experiences with the porters and clerks. At last he gained entrance and delivered his message. He related how he had seen the Lady again, and this time there were tears in his eyes. And now the heart of the humble Franciscan prelate no longer doubted the story. But without visible proof, what would his powerful enemies say? Thus far the King's men in New Spain had shamefully slandered and hounded the poor bishop for shielding the natives from their greed. Now they would say that the aging Zumárraga, who had represented the Holy Office both in Spain and in the New World, had embraced the superstitions of an ignorant Indian. This prompted him to bid Juan Diego to ask the Lady for a sign, a token that could be seen. What sign? Any sign; they would leave that up to her.

To increase the number of witnesses, the bishop assigned two men of his household to follow the Indian and report on what they saw. This was a slip of judgment on his part, in that the Lady had chosen to confide only in Juan Diego and himself at this time. And so, as Juan Diego crossed a small stream near the base of Tepeyac, his two spies lost sight of him, and came back saying that the Indian was a cheat or, what was worse, a dealer in witchcraft.

And Juan Diego, ignorant of his being followed or of his act of vanishing, kept on plodding to the top of Tepeyac where the Lady was waiting. He told her about his latest audience with the bishop and about the request for a token, and she very tenderly thanked him for his faithfulness, promising to give him the sign on the following day.

Arriving home, he found his aged uncle, Juan Bernardino, very ill with a fever. This man, also newly baptized, had likewise gotten both a Spanish name and surname, and his nephew loved him dearly as his foster father. Juan Diego passed the night and all next morning ministering to him. The rest of the day, Monday the eleventh, was spent in looking for a herb doctor and in bringing him over to see the sick man. In spite of all this care, Juan Bernardino grew steadily worse by nightfall, and then he begged his nephew to set out early next morning to fetch a Father confessor at the friary of Tlatelolco.

Tuesday, December the twelfth, again at daybreak, and exactly as it had happened on Saturday, Juan Diego found himself about to climb the east slope of Tepeyac, when his slow wits recalled that he had utterly forgotten about his promise to meet the Lady the day before. Now what would she say? He decided to take another path, one much longer around the base of the hill, taking care that he could not be seen from the rocky ridge above. But then, as he made the last turn, he saw her coming toward him.

"Where are you going, my child?" she asked chidingly. "And what road is this that you have taken?"

Juan Diego hung his head, and humbly gave his excuse, his

very sick uncle who had been like a father to him. Even now he was on his way to get one of the priests to assist him in his last hour. At first he must have found it hard to believe when she told him not to worry, for his uncle would not die; in fact, he was already hale and sound. For had she not come to comfort his people? Then Juan Diego took her words with joy, and promptly asked her for the sign so that he might take it to the bishop without further delay.

And again she said something unbelievable. She told him to climb the hill and gather some roses growing there, and to bring them back to her. Now Juan Diego knew that December was not the time for flowers, much less roses, and that rocky Tepeyac was no place for roses at any season. But he went without doubting her word and found the hilltop abloom with sweet-scented roses, rare roses of Castile, fresh and fragrant and bepearled with dewdrops. These he plucked and dropped into his *tilma* — a long cloth of woven fiber that all ordinary Indians of that region wore tied around their neck. As a shield from sun and rain, it usually hung like a cape over the back. But to gather things, like maize or melons, it was pulled to the front like a great bib, and its lower end was held up to form a large pouch. In this manner, Juan Diego took a mantleful of roses to Mary, still waiting where he had met her this fourth time.

She lifted the bunch of roses in both her lovely hands, and then gently placed them back in the *tilma,* explaining that this was the sign he was to give the bishop, and that he must show them to no one along the way. Juan Diego started off in his short-stepped Indian run to the city of Mexico, from time to time taking a quick look at the roses or sniffing their sweet smell as he went.

The bishop's servants were no less haughty than before. Now they were likewise curious to know what Juan Diego carried, and he had to struggle with his shoulders and elbows to protect his secret burden. But thrice, at the least, the rude familiars of his lordship managed to see what appeared to them like roses painted or embroidered on the coarsely woven cloth. This they reported to their master.

Fray Juan de Zumárraga, barefooted in his rough Franciscan robe and knotted cord, and flanked by his stern secretaries, called out a kind welcome when the Indian came in, and Juan Diego, announcing that he brought the sign, let go the ends of his mantle without further ado. Out rolled the roses upon the stone floor, and the bishop sank speechless to his knees. The roses were miracle enough, indeed. But that picture on the *tilma* drew forth his very soul through his staring eyes. It was truly Mary conceived without sin, the Woman clothed with the sun and the moon beneath her feet. His first action was to kiss the mantle's hem humbly and tenderly; then, rising to his feet, he undid the knot at the nape of Juan Diego's hairy neck and devoutly carried the holy painting to the altar of his private oratory.

Juan Diego slept that night in the bishop's house, where he was made to tell his story over and over again. Next day he accompanied the bishop and other witnesses to Tepeyac, where he showed them the very spots where the Lady had stood and spoken to him. Then he begged leave to go and see his uncle Juan Bernardino. Wishing to check on this part of the story, the bishop dispatched some of his familiars with him to the hills, while he stayed behind with the others to discuss the chapel to be built.

The other party found Juan Bernardino most happy in his restored health, and also most eager to tell how it all came about. The Lady, he said, looking just as Juan Diego had described her, came and cured him; and it was at daybreak, when she had last spoken to his nephew. Furthermore, she told him that her name was "Santa Maria de Guadalupe."

Thereupon, both Juan Diego and Juan Bernardino were taken back to the bishop, and he took them on to his own house, where they were his guests for many days, until the little adobe chapel was built by the large flocks of Indians who soon had caught the ever-spreading good news. For while Juan Diego and his companions had gone to see about his uncle, Fray Juan de Zumárraga had outlined with his own hand the place where the first little chapel's walls were to rise. And when it was finished in short order, his lordship and great throngs bore the sacred image in solemn procession from the city of Mexico to Tepeyac.

If I have bored you by recounting this well-known happening in its every detail, I myself have greatly enjoyed retelling it. For it was a tremendous event that changed the course of men's lives and fortunes in New Spain and the Indies, both Indians and Spaniards. That the latter did not take this manifestation to their hearts for a long, long time is also a part of my own life's story, and will be told in its place among other related things.

Zacatecas was our next major halting place, a bustling young city in the midst of feverishly worked mines of gold and silver. Tepeyac and the city of Mexico were three weeks and three hundred and fifty miles behind us, but our goal still lay much further ahead, some eight hundred and fifty and more miles of rugged and mostly uninhabited country.

A hundred and sixty miles further north we came to a place that was later called Durango, a small wild town also in mining country. But Father Alonso de Benavides kept the caravan pushing on for two hundred more miles until we reached Santa Barbara and the Parral district. This was the frontier of New Spain, where only a few Spaniards worked the mines with Indian labor and raised cattle in vast haciendas. Beyond lay great stretches of level plains and desert, crisscrossed by huge sharp mountains of treeless stone. As delegate of the Holy Office, Father Alonso had to spend some months here, on cases entrusted to him by the authorities before we left the city of Mexico.

Perhaps it was just as well that we waited for autumn before going ahead. The hot summer months would have taxed the endurance of men and beasts alike. Here the valleys were green and pleasant even in July and August. I noticed how Father Alonso and the captain of the escorting soldiers used to spend long evenings together, sometimes with Governor Sotelo present, talking in low tones about conditions in the kingdom of New Mexico, which was the homeland of this captain, Francisco Gómez, and my own home for centuries to come.

## CHAPTER II

CAPTAIN Francisco Gómez was a Portuguese soldier, well built and handsome, with a rather serious countenance and a vague, let us say, Jewish cast of features. He had been born in a suburb of Lisbon, and after both his parents died, was reared under the eye of a much older brother, or half brother, who was a Franciscan priest. Later, a Spanish nobleman by the name of Oñate took the boy as his page to the Court of Madrid, and from there, several years later, his master brought him along to the New World. From New Spain, Francisco went north to the new colony in New Mexico, which had been established there in 1598 by the nobleman's brother, Don Juan de Oñate.

Young Gómez was a good military man and a leader, and he quickly rose to the rank of captain. He was also given an *encomienda;* that is, an Indian pueblo was entrusted to his rule and care. With his title of *encomendero* he had the right to levy taxes, and also the obligation to draft Indian warriors and lead them into battle whenever the Spanish colonists and the Pueblo Indians were threatened by hostile heathen tribes. He had the further duty to see that his Indians were properly catechized, and to protect them from abuse by the white man.

In these matters, the captain had much to say to Father Alonso de Benavides. Some unscrupulous Spanish governors, from 1610 when Santa Fe was founded to the present year of 1625, had practiced slave labor on the Indians for their own personal gain. Some of the local *encomenderos* had done the same, instead of living up to their duties as guardians of their Indians in the King's name. Such abuses had ignited scandalous quarrels among government officials and the mission Fathers, and sometimes this or that Father made matters worse by his own rashness. This was the state of affairs that Father Alonso would find when he reached Santa Fe. At present he formed no judgments, but laid these things away for future guidance. Nevertheless, he did make up his mind as to the staunch character of Francisco Gómez, and I myself liked the captain, too, knowing that he also would love me after I was unpacked and enthroned in the parish church of Santa Fe.

We aimed straight north some days after leaving the Parral area, trading a land of rivers and green valleys for two hundred and fifty miles of a merciless Sahara that drained gasps and groans from men and animals for many days. At last we came in sight of what Captain Gómez had been mentioning very often of late — El Paso del Río del Norte. There was nothing here, not even a hut, only a swift brown river breaking through a pass among bare sugar-loaf mountains to the north that reminded me of giant pedestals. But the sight of barely green grass and leafless cottonwoods along the banks was like a paradise to the desert travelers. A wonderful site for a great city, I thought, somehow feeling that I would see this spot again someday. And one of those great bluffs, thought I again, would make a grand pedestal for a gigantic statue of the Savior, Christ the King of all creation.

Those very bluffs, the captain told the friars, were the gateway to the kingdom of New Mexico and the Franciscan Custody of the Conversion of St. Paul. But Santa Fe still lay more than three hundred miles further north, where the sierras were deep green and blue and purple, according to the season or the time of day, and their peaks white all winter long, or crimson many a day at sunset, as though with the blood of holy friars slain in times gone by.

After fording the river at El Paso del Norte, our caravan

of ox-drawn carts and people on horseback passed through the narrow defile of barren stone peaks into another large valley. Fortunately, the stream was low early in December, and the ox train did not have much trouble crossing. The weather, too, was becoming cooler, not only because we were going further north each day, but on account of the land's steady rise, which could be seen in the river's rapid rush. Hence its name Río Bravo del Norte, which means Fierce River of the North. Its present name of Rio Grande, although Spanish, was applied to it centuries later by map makers from the former English colonies far to the east.

About fifty miles north of the ford the valley narrowed again, as if the surrounding desert wanted to choke it to death. Here the captain pointed out a great round-shouldered bluff on the west side of the river which was known as Mount Robledo. At this spot on the trail, twenty-seven years before, old Pedro Robledo of Toledo had died; he was buried on Corpus Christi Day, May the twenty-first, in the year 1598. He was the first member of Oñate's colony to die in New Mexico. Captain Gómez made sure that all the newcomers clearly understood that old Robledo was his wife's grandfather. And I myself must say here that I am purposely tarrying in describing the land, and certain happenings, because it is all part and parcel of my story. This itinerary has to be remembered if my future adventures are to be fully appreciated.

From here the river veered more and more to the west; but again the captain led the ox train directly north over a long stretch of desert, just as he had done further south when we left the Parral country. He explained that the winding river valley would make the journey much longer; besides, countless deep arroyos and great gravel hills on the west side, and bare ranges of steep mountains close to the east bank, made travel by cart impossible. He also assured Father Alonso and the governor that this trek was less than a hundred miles until we came upon the river once more, and that he and his soldiers knew every inch of it.

Many years after this my journey, it came to be known as the Jornada del Muerto, or the Dead Man's Route, when the Spaniards found the remains of a wandering German peddler who had perished on his way south to the city of Mexico.

We made this perilous stretch safely, and sooner than we the newcomers expected, for the oxen kept moving steadily in the increasingly cool weather. At one point before we again met the river, as we approached a great table mountain of black lava, like a mammoth pancake burnt black at the edges, I saw a single white cloud hanging motionless many miles to the east. And I thought of another cloud that would hover above that spot three hundred and twenty years later — a cloud shaped like a giant mushroom and casting invisible death for leagues around the flats of Alamogordo.

Days later we reached the southernmost of the Indian pueblos, or villages made of mud two and more stories high. One of these, which belonged to the Piros tribe, was called Socorro by the Spaniards, because these kind Indians had succored the needy Oñate colonists with generous gifts of bread and maize. I mention this place with feeling, for not long after our arrival Father Alonso had a mission established there under the title that I represented, Our Lady of the Assumption. I like to think that he did it because of me. Years later people shortened the name by referring to the mission as Our Lady of Socorro, which has misled later folks into thinking that it was dedicated in honor of Our Lady of Perpetual Help. This last title comes from a Byzantine painting long venerated in a church in Rome, but unknown outside of Italy at this period.

We passed other southern pueblos, among them Alamillo and Sevilleta, where Captain Gómez proudly showed us his *encomienda* and his hacienda of Las Barrancas. I could see that his Indians loved and respected him. The further north we went, the more frequent were these Indian villages, with Spanish haciendas scattered in between them, for the land was more fertile and pleasant in every way. Finally, some days before Christmas, we arrived at the Queres pueblo of Santo Domingo, headquarters for all the missions, and here Father Alonso was to reside. Most of the carts, carrying supplies for the missions, stopped to unload here. Those with the governor's effects, and others destined for Santa Fe, continued on the last lap of thirty miles to the capital and only Spanish town, where the governor was to be welcomed with great pomp and ceremony, where Captain Francisco Gómez would embrace his beloved wife and children once more.

I went along, too, with other boxes containing sections of a small altar reredos, a large crucifix, several rolled paintings on canvas — all, like myself, destined for the parish church of the Assumption. And so I reached my new home at last, after twelve hundred rough miles on a lurching cart.

Father Alonso de Benavides waited a whole month before coming up to Santa Fe. Not only did he give Governor Sotelo time to get properly settled, and also to prepare the capital for a worthy reception of the new head of the missions, and the first delegate of the Holy Office besides, but he selected a significant day for the occasion. It was the feast of the Conversion of St. Paul, the twenty-fifth day of January, which was the titular feast of the missions, officially known as the Franciscan Custody of the Conversion of St. Paul. Father Alonso arrived in Santa Fe the evening before the feast day and was met by the governor and his Council, followed by all the citizens. The entire garrison paraded forth under the royal standard of the kingdom, which displayed the embroidered image of Our Lady of Remedies upon it. Amid salvos from harquebuses and the artillery, Father Alonso was conducted to the friary, and the next morning a most colorful Solemn Mass was chanted in the church of the Assumption. In all these ceremonies, while the governor's aide-de-camp carried the royal standard, the man appointed by Father Alonso to bear the great standard of the Holy Office was none other than Francisco Gómez, now promoted to *sargento mayor,* or major.

From this time on things fared well and smoothly, and a new spirit took hold of the people at large. A major work ordered at once by Father Alonso was the razing of the fifteen-year-old church, which was merely a temporary structure, and which he called a shanty, and the immediate building of a larger church of adobe. Here he enthroned me, to be admired not only by the Spanish people and the Indians who came in from the pueblos, but even by Apache chieftains from the faraway plains who came to see me and afterward asked Father Alonso to send missionaries among their people.

The already established missions also flared up with new vigor, while new ones were founded in the pueblos that had none so far. Among these was Our Lady of the Assumption at Socorro Pueblo. Other missions dedicated in Mary's honor were as follows: Our Lady of the Assumption at Zia Pueblo, the Immaculate Conception at Cuarac Pueblo and also at Hawikuh Pueblo in Zuñi, Our Lady of the Angels at Pecos Pueblo, and Our Lady's Nativity at Chilili Pueblo. Thirty years later two more missions of Mary were to be born: Our Lady of the Purification at Halona Pueblo in Zuñi and — remember it well — Our Lady of Guadalupe away down south at the first crossing of our river, at El Paso del Río del Norte.

During Father Alonso's three-year term, relations between the Fathers and the Spanish officials were most cordial, even though some malcontents tried to disrupt the harmony by ruses that the priest handled with tact. Social life, too, beamed with happiness and with color in spite of frontier conditions. I recall especially the birth of Francisco Gómez Robledo, child of Francisco Gómez and Ana Robledo. His godparents were Governor

Sotelo and Doña Isabel de Bohorques, wife of the general commander of troops, Don Pedro Durán y Chávez. And when young Francisco was confirmed shortly afterward by Father Alonso, the same governor stood as sponsor. If I recall this particular occasion, it is because this boy grew up to be my knight and champion.

After more than three years in the kingdom of New Mexico and the Custody of the Conversion of St. Paul, Fray Alonso de Benavides left us when the supply ox train departed for New Spain in the fall of 1629. The following year he wrote a *Memorial* describing the missions of New Mexico, their great problems and greater possibilities. This was presented to the King of Spain, was printed in Madrid, and soon was being translated and published in various countries of Europe. Three years later he wrote a revision of it at the request of Pope Urban VIII. In both works, Father Alonso makes special mention of me.

These *Memorials,* and other letters that he wrote, show that he yearned to return to us with all his heart, to carry out his great dream of missionary endeavor. Some people have thought that he was a self-seeking man, because he exaggerated the number of Indians and also proposed that a bishopric be established in New Mexico. But I know that he was using official figures in an age when populations were more guessed at than counted. I also know that if he had been sent back to us as a bishop, his dignity and authority would have quelled many sad happenings that plagued our kingdom for centuries after. The Golden Age of our missions, which he so auspiciously started, would have gone on to full brilliance in his lifetime as our first bishop, instead of whirling off in dust clouds in the decades after he was gone.

The authorities in Europe did think him worthy of being a bishop, but sent him elsewhere, to Goa in Portuguese India, far across the seas and the world. But he never got there; I had wanted him for New Mexico.

## CHAPTER III

DOÑA Ana Robledo was only twenty-five years old when I first came to Santa Fe. She was small, and her delicate look belied that valiant woman of the Scriptures who is the pride of her husband and family. After her grandfather's death by Mount Robledo in 1598, her grandmother with her four soldier sons and two daughters had pushed on north with Oñate's colonists to found the first Spanish settlement at Yunque, or San Gabriel, where the Chama River joins the Río Bravo del Norte near San Juan Pueblo.

One of the two daughters, Luisa, was already married to a young Toledo countryman, Lieutenant Bartolomé Romero. There in San Gabriel, their daughter Ana opened her little blue eyes, one of the first Spanish children to be born in New Mexico. And not too many years later, after Santa Fe was founded, the young girl married the dashing but serious newcomer from Portugal, Francisco Gómez.

They had seven children in all, among them a girl, Francisca, and two boys that come into my life, Francisco and Andrés. In that small northernmost outpost of the Spanish Empire which was Santa Fe, when the rest of upper North America was unknown, save for small spots far away toward the Atlantic coast, Ana Robledo and her husband taught their children letters. This was over and above the vital knowledge and skills needed in a day when girls marrying in their early teens had to make a home out of things at hand, when lads of twelve were considered grown soldiers as well as hard-riding hunters and cattlemen. Ana learned by constant use to temper and bear a mother's anxiety, for seldom were all her men at home at one time. Always, her husband or one or more of the boys were out on an Indian campaign, or a bison hunt on the great plains, or else far down south directing the affairs of their father's *encomienda*. No matter where they were outside of Santa Fe, their lives were always in grave peril.

In later years there was her dear husband's ever-growing silent bitterness, never once spent on her, but which she felt because of their closeness. Through his sheer powers as a man and a soldier, Francisco Gómez had become the most important man in the kingdom. Each succeeding governor relied on his judgment, and this opened every door of the Palace of the Governors to his wife and family. But Gómez was disliked by the other colonists for being an outsider, and because he kept aloof from opposing factions whose petty intrigues varied with the weather. Even some of the mission Fathers, who rashly allied themselves with this or that party, worked against him.

Rumors were spread about that Gómez not only had Jewish blood but also practiced Judaism in secret — circumcizing his sons and saying prayers on Friday while wearing a cap inside the house. It was a ruse to ruin him by having him arrested by the Holy Office and recalled to the city of Mexico for a trial which could last for years. The purpose of the Holy Office, you see, was to root out subversion in Church and State; it had no jurisdiction over Jews or heretics as such, not even over heathen Indians, but only over Catholics. Hence, it could and did try baptized converts who secretly had clung to their former allegiance. It was presumed that they had become Catholics for sinister purposes. Rumors of this sort failed to result in Gómez' arrest, but they did bring unhappiness to those concerned.

Such was the ignorance of the populace in these matters that many testified to the Judaism of the Gómez Robledo boys because they were supposed to have little tails. The fact is that one of the sons (some said Juan, others said Francisco) had an abnormal coccyx which was noticed when as children they bathed in the little Santa Fe river. This tiny bone at the end of the spine stuck out instead of curling inward and out of sight under the skin, as with most people. Now all the men of the family were supposed to have this appendage and were disdainfully referred to as *"Los Colitas."* Deeply hurt by this and other displays of envy and ill will, the father stood by each governor sent from New Spain, even when some of these committed outrages against the people and the missions.

In 1641, when dying shortly after his arrival, Governor Flores appointed Francisco Gómez as acting governor of the kingdom in compliance with royal law. But the Council, which was made up of local colonists, defied the royal decrees by refusing to accept him. Gómez died some fourteen years later, not too much embittered, since he was consoled by the mettle of his grown family and most especially by the staunch faithfulness and piety of his wife. And Ana Robledo lived on for many years, and some of her children also, to be further knitted into my life's story. For I have dwelt this much on the Gómez Robledo family because I was part of it, from the day I arrived in Santa Fe with Francisco Gómez in 1625, as you shall see.

There was a Confraternity of the Immaculate Conception in Santa Fe which was in existence when I came. Practically all of the citizens belonged to it, and they observed the major feasts of Our Lady with solemn Vespers the evening before and a procession through the streets flaring bright with *luminarias,* little bonfires of fragrant piñon wood. On the feastday itself there was a Mass with another procession. The costs of these celebrations were borne by the society's funds, which consisted of dues and gifts made in textile goods, elk skins and bison hides, and even livestock. I remember very well when Governor Rosas, a most wicked man, confiscated a very fine mule which a member gave to the Confraternity.

After my arrival, it was I who was taken out in procession as Our Lady's representation, so that within a few years both I and the parish church came to be known as Our Lady of the Conception. The change came about in this way.

The dogma of the Immaculate Conception had been promulgated for the Spanish kingdoms in the year 1617, so the people were freshly and deeply imbued with this heavenly view of Mary. Many of the Spanish Franciscans, including those in the kingdom of New Mexico, were wearing blue because of this, instead of gray or brown. At this period a gifted painter in Seville, Murillo by name, was painting a score of Immaculate Conceptions that have since become world-famous. And because the spiritual idea of the Immaculate Conception cannot be depicted of itself, the works of Murillo, and of other painters and sculptors who imitated him, were based on the already familiar images of the Assumption of Our Lady — the Virgin among clouds and upheld by angels.

And so this change of title was no trouble, and most natural, as far as it concerned me. With a crescent of silver attached to my pedestal, I as an actress had changed my role.

However, other changes followed which went much deeper. While the parish church kept its title of the Immaculate Conception, the Confraternity and I changed to Our Lady of the Rosary; but for me it was much more than the mere switch of title.

First of all, this turning to Mary as Our Lady of the Rosary came about when the roving heathen Indians became bolder in attacking the Spanish colonists and the Christian Pueblo Indians; the menace grew so bad that eventually the Salinas pueblos east of the Manzano Mountains, and their great mission churches of stone, had to be abandoned. These Indians were removed to Socorro and other related southern pueblos on the Río del Norte. When threatened by fierce enemies from without, the Spanish people were accustomed to pray to Mary under her title of the Rosary, and this custom arose from the victory of the Spanish fleet over the Saracens at Lepanto in the year 1571, the first Sunday of October, when the Confraternity of the Rosary in Rome went through the streets praying for victory over an enemy that threatened to overrun Christian Europe.

And now to my change in appearance for this new role. By this time it had also become a general custom, in Spain as well as her New World colonies, to dress sacred images in real clothes. We would call it a fad today. All statues of Mary, no matter what her particular title, came to be dressed like Spanish Queens, with jeweled crowns and with silken gowns and mantles of royalty. I was taken from the altar one day, and someone began slicing off my shoulders, until my arms down to the elbows were completely gone. Then in front they broke off my folded hands, and began paring away my forearms and much of my bosom; they also cut away the thick folds of my mantle at my waist all around. The bare yellow wood looked sickly pale in contrast with my rich arabesque garments below, for I was not touched from the waist down. Luckily, traces of my upper garments were left on my back and shoulders, and the upper part of my breast, so that observing persons centuries later could easily find out how I had looked originally as the Assumption of Mary.

Next they drove crude iron hooks into my armless shoulders, and from them hung shapeless arms that moved also at the elbows, like those of a puppet. The new hands at the end of them were more finished, but their poise was awkward. Little pierced iron wedges were hammered into my ear lobes, to hold earrings. And they drove a hole into the top of my head; this was to receive a small spike that held my crown in place.

From an actress to a puppet — what a deep humiliation, I thought. A real flesh-and-blood lady would have died, of course, from such severe mutilations. But even granting that she had felt no pain and lost no blood, she would have died much sooner from shame and mortally wounded vanity.

However, after Ana Robledo and other women came and slipped my new clumsy arms through little silken sleeves, and covered me with a brocade mantle trimmed with gold, and then fitted a golden crown on my head, I felt greatly relieved. And when other gowns and capes of every color began to arrive, and other crowns, and strings of pearls and colored beads, and even jeweled earrings, I began to be glad that they had spoiled my original beauty. For the chopped waist and the clumsy arms could not be seen under the clothing. And what woman, even one made out of wood, would not prefer an extensive and varied wardrobe to a single dress, even one made of gold leaf?

So, in my solitary dreams I began to be grateful to Our Lady of Guadalupe, not the holy painting in the Valley of Mexico, but a much older statue in Spain, for my present fortune, since it is through her that this fad began.

After Spain was converted to Christianity by the Apostle St. James, the country went through Roman persecutions and later Gothic invasions, as did Italy. And, like Christian Italy, she later flourished to such a degree that she furnished a Pope and many doctors to the early Church, while very important Councils were held in Spanish cities. But after the year 700, the Saracens from North Africa invaded her shores and gradually drove the Christians up into the northern mountains of the peninsula. Many of these fleeing people hid their most prized statues before the conquering Moors took their cities and towns. Six hundred years later, after the Moors were driven back to the southern coast of Spain, several of these fine crucifixes and Madonnas were found, and they have been venerated ever since in numerous shrines throughout that thoroughly Catholic land.

One of these famous Virgins is Our Lady of Guadalupe. It is a seated figure of wood, about my own height, representing Mary with her Child on her left arm. The surface, darkened by the ages, is the color of slate. It was found in the thirteenth century by a peasant of Cáceres in Extremadura, who was looking for a stray cow in a high range of mountains, to which the now-expelled Moors had given the name of Guadalupe. According to the ancient legend, the Blessed Virgin appeared to this man and told him to get his parish priest and fellow townsmen to come and dig at this spot, where they would find her image, and build a shrine for it. The clergy and people of Cáceres unearthed a tomb of the early Christian era, and in it found the statue hidden. From the stones of the tomb and other buried ruins they built the first primitive shrine, which was later replaced by better chapels. And it is recorded, as early as the year 1337, that the Cardinal Archbishop of Seville proudly considered himself the rector of this shrine, around which a town had grown, and where King Alfonso XI had built an imposing church.

In the year 1340 this Alfonso won a great victory over Albohacen, the ruler of Morocco, after imploring the help of Our Lady of Guadalupe, and this made her shrine the center of devotion in the Iberian peninsula. And after Ferdinand and Isabella gave the final blow to the Moors at Santa Fe near Granada in 1492, and the treasures of the Incas and the Aztecs began to flow into the Spanish royal coffers following the discovery of America, such great gifts were showered on Guadalupe that the image had crowns of pure gold, and wore mantles and dresses of gold and silver thread embroidered with pearls from the Indies. Whether or not the fashion of dressing statues of Mary began at this period, or much earlier, does not matter; but it is here that it started, and it is to this Spanish Guadalupe that I owe my present regal attire.

Now, Guadalupe (which in Moorish Arabic means "hidden river") lies in the extreme western part of New Castile, and hence was known as the province of Extremadura. This was the birthplace of Pizarro and Cortés and most of the first conquistadores of the New World — and of my kingdom of New Mexico. Though peasants, most of them, they knew that they were descended from knights who had vanquished the Moors, that their history and ancestry were intimately tied up with the famous knightly Order of Santiago. And so they were haughty as well as brave, unafraid of hardships that led to glory, but afraid of common labor. (This is the one and only true reason for their enslavement of the poor Indians.)

Because these *extremeños* were also extremely devoted to their Lady of Guadalupe back home, it is believed, and with good reason, that when the Indian Juan Bernardino said that the Lady of Tepeyac had called herself "St. Mary of Guadalupe," this was what these Spaniards heard, and not what the Indian actually said. The Spaniards changed Aztec words to Isabella gave the final blow to the Moors at Santa Fe near Granada in 1492, and the treasures of the Incas and the Aztecs began to flow into the Spanish royal coffers following the discovery of America, such great gifts were showered on Guadalupe that the image had crowns of pure gold, and wore mantles and dresses of gold and silver thread embroidered with pearls from the Indies. Whether or not the fashion of dressing statues of Mary began at this period, or much earlier, does not matter; but it is here that it started, and it is to this Spanish Guadalupe that I owe my present regal attire.

Now, Guadalupe (which in Moorish Arabic means "hidden river") lies in the extreme western part of New Castile, and hence was known as the province of Extremadura. This was the birthplace of Pizarro and Cortés and most of the first conquistadores of the New World — and of my kingdom of

New Mexico. Though peasants, most of them, they knew that they were descended from knights who had vanquished the Moors, that their history and ancestry were intimately tied up with the famous knightly Order of Santiago. And so they were haughty as well as brave, unafraid of hardships that led to glory, but afraid of common labor. (This is the one and only true reason for their enslavement of the poor Indians.)

Because these *extremeños* were also extremely devoted to their Lady of Guadalupe back home, it is believed, and with good reason, that when the Indian Juan Bernardino said that the Lady of Tepeyac had called herself "St. Mary of Guadalupe," this was what these Spaniards heard, and not what the Indian actually said. The Spaniards changed Aztec words to time. Afterward Peñalosa defended himself before the Holy Office against much more serious crimes by boasting that he himself had given me not only a veil and crown, but also a rosary and some of his most prized plumes — the liar! I loathe to mention some of these evil governors by name, but they have to be brought into my story to date important incidents, just as the name of Pontius Pilate found its way into the Apostles' Creed.

Alas, for my poor, dear, brave Ana. Not only were her many years steeped in troubles and anxieties, but her last ones on earth were further burdened and saddened when her son Francisco was arrested by the Holy Office and hauled off to jail in the city of Mexico, because of the old rumors about the family that had now burst into open charges.

## CHAPTER IV

FRANCISCO Gómez Robledo was a big man, red-bearded and hearty. Over and above the brave qualities inherited from his father, he had a bold fighting spirit that must have come from Ana Robledo. Instead of silently brooding over underhanded attacks, he fought back with telling effect. His foes took the last resort of cowards by formally denouncing him to the Holy Office of the Inquisition for a Judaizing Christian, as, they said, his late father had also been. It was an ironic turn, for well I remembered how his valiant father had carried the banner of the Holy Office the day Father Benavides was received in Santa Fe more than forty years before.

His enemies envied the superior powers that had won him high military rank as well as civil position in government. And they were cut to the quick, even some friars, when in defending himself he pointed out their real defects. Perhaps they were envious, too, of all the family had done for me. Francisco, especially, loved to assist his mother in matters of my wardrobe and my shrine. He had also been the *mayordomo* or president of my Confraternity these many years before his arrest in 1661; in fact, he held this office even during his imprisonment and trial. Rough and ready otherwise, he was delicately gentle when dressing me. This is not to say that he was a saint, for he had been a very wild boy.

Francisco was kept in the Inquisition's jail in the city of Mexico for three years, during which time he was brought several times before the tribunal of the Holy Office. He answered all questions straightforwardly and without fear.

Without irreverence, but boldly, he threw back the accusations into the faces of his accusers. Almost comically he pointed out how some of his examiners had but the vaguest idea concerning circumcision. And all the while he displayed his manly devotion to Mary through me and the Lady of Tepeyac. In the end he was acquitted with honor. He returned to Santa Fe to continue in his high military and civic offices, and also as the president of my Confraternity down to the year 1684, as though nothing had happened. But from then on he was greatly respected by all and sundry. No one spoke or thought ill any more of old Francisco Gómez or of his brave family.

Francisco's return as a vindicated hero not only gladdened the heart of his aged mother, but shed new brilliance on his living brethren. His sister Francisca, for several years married to Pedro Lucero de Godoy, had a numerous family that was fast gaining prominence. His two surviving brothers, Andrés and Bartolomé, could not be stopped now in their rise toward political and military influence. And my Confraternity of the Holy Rosary waxed stronger, all its members ever more devoted to me, their little Queen and Conquistadora.

At this particular period my people had become strongly aware of their ancestry, perhaps because there was not much else to boast about. The meagerest excuse was needed for them to recall their parents and grandparents as founders and conquistadores of their kingdom. And since I had come in their day, I was also one of the conquerors. However, this unique title or nickname for an image of Mary was not altogether new. The word itself had originated in the Cortés conquest of Mexico, and it could be that Francisco Gómez Robledo brought back the idea from his forced sojourn in the city of Mexico.

The first Conquistadora is a small statue of Our Lady of the Angels, known also afterward as Our Lady of Remedies, which Cortés had with him in the conquest of Mexico City. He gave it to Acxotecatl, a Tlaxcaltec chieftain, who in turn gave it to Fray Juan de Ribas, one of the Franciscan "Twelve Apostles" of New Spain. Father Ribas took it to the new city of Puebla de los Angeles, where a magnificent shrine was built for it on the ancient pagan temple pyramid of Cholula. At the time Gómez Robledo was in the city of Mexico her popularity was at its height, and a book was being printed in which proof was given that this was a true Conquistadora, that is, an image of Mary that had come in Cortés' Army together with that of Our Lady of Remedies, which is in the Valley of Mexico itself.

This other Remedios statue, with her own popular shrine and following in the Valley of Mexico, also comes into my life, as will be seen shortly when we again encounter that royal standard of the kingdom of New Mexico which went out to meet Father Benavides in 1626.

## CHAPTER V

SIXTEEN years after Francisco Gómez Robledo's triumphant return from the city of Mexico, and almost fifty-five since my own coming to Santa Fe, a horrible calamity befell my kingdom of New Mexico and its royal capital. The storm clouds had been steadily gathering all this while, since Father Alonso de Benavides left, what with so many bad governors who exploited the poor Pueblo Indians, not to speak of the abuses and un-Christian example set by many of the local leaders. One or the other of the friars, too, had by their misdeeds helped to undo the work of loving sacrifice of scores of other sons of St. Francis.

On the tenth of August, in the year 1680, the secretly united pueblos struck. It was the feast of St. Lawrence, the first Spanish martyr. Twenty-one holy and devoted Padres died on that day, as also several defenseless families living in their haciendas away from Santa Fe.

Only six years before a strange warning had been given. Following a severe drought between the years 1667 and 1672, that had brought widespread suffering among Indians and Spanish folk alike, a ten-year-old girl of Santa Fe had made a disturbing prophecy. While ill with a fever, she had commended herself to the holy Virgin; and in her distress she dreamed that a little image of Our Lady of the Blessed Sacrament in her room (the original statue and shrine are in Toledo) cured her and then said to her: "Daughter, rise up and announce that the Custody will soon be destroyed because of the lack of reverence it has for my priests, and that this miracle will be testimony of the truth; and that the people must make amends for their guilt unless they wish to be punished further."

The girl rose up cured from her bed, and when her message was spread abroad things took a turn for the better. People who had written false complaints against the friars to send to New Spain tore up the letters. Peace and good will began to flourish between certain officials and the missionaries. But the medicinemen in the pueblos had already made up their minds. Moreover, it had been foretold that the destruction was coming for sure, whether the people repented or not. However, because a sincere effort was made at betterment in these six years, most of the colonists escaped with their lives.

On the ninth of August, Francisco Gómez Robledo was sent by Governor Otermin to bring in two Indian suspects from the nearby pueblo of Tesuque, because warnings had already come about the Indians planning a general uprising on the thirteenth. The governor also sent messages to the Fathers and captains in the several pueblos to be on the alert. But on the tenth, other officers and soldiers began to trickle into the capital from every direction, with the sad news that the Indians were already on the warpath and many of the Fathers were dead.

Otermin then sent Francisco with a squadron to the haciendas at La Cañada, north of Santa Fe; he returned on the twelfth to report that the north Tewa Indians had massacred several Padres and some families, had desecrated the mission churches, and then had fled to the mountains. His party killed one Indian scout who would not give himself up but, as he told them boldly, preferred to die and go to hell. The following day news came from the south that all the Spanish colonists there were dead. Knowing that soon the capital itself would be attacked, the governor advised the Santa Fe Fathers to consume the Blessed Sacrament and have all sacred vessels and images removed from the parish church to the fortresslike Palace of the Governors and its adjoining garrison. The next day brought news that the pueblos of the Galisteo Basin and the Pecos were approaching slowly from the south, waiting for other Indians to join them, including their own lifelong enemies, the Apaches. They attacked Santa Fe on the fifteenth, in the morning. Many of the warriors had Spanish swords and muskets. Their chief, on horseback and dressed with all the arms of some dead Spaniard, including a red sash that had recently been the missal veil at the mission of Galisteo, was induced to parley with the governor. But all to no avail. The chief falsely announced that all the colonists of the southern district were dead, and said that it was now the capital's turn to perish. With this he ordered an attack, and his warriors set fire to the chapel of San Miguel on the south side of the river. The defenders of Santa Fe then poured out to engage them in combat. It was a daylong battle. Many Indians were killed and some Spaniards wounded. Toward evening the attackers were almost completely routed, and the soldiers were collecting recaptured horses and firearms, when a horde of northern Pueblo fighters arrived to attack the town from the other side. This was the beginning of a siege which lasted for nine days, with defenders and attackers fighting back and forth every day.

During this time the Indian warriors increased in number, while the besieged people, now herded into the courtyard of the palace and garrison, began to suffer greatly from thirst. For the Indians had diverted the clear stream that ran close by from springs and a meadow beyond the parish church. And by now they had occupied all the houses around the palace, and had set fire to the church which had been my own palace and throne for more than half a century.

On the twentieth of August, at sunrise, the governor and his men made one final, desperate counterassault, having invoked my aid with special prayers the night before. Calling

43

the name of her whom I unworthily represent, the small Spanish force slowly but steadily dislodged the enemy from the houses. By the end of the day more than three hundred Indians lay dead, forty-seven were captured, and the other fifteen hundred of every pueblo and nation were in flight.

Only four of our soldiers were killed, and one officer. But this officer was Andrés Gómez Robledo, Francisco's brother. He left a young widow, Juana Ortiz Baca, and their six little daughters. These girls were to glorify me someday as their parents and grandparents had done before them.

The Fathers of Santa Fe persuaded the governor to abandon the capital, for of the thousand and more souls in the palace compound, less than a hundred were professional men of arms. And the enemy was sure to return in greater numbers after they had danced themselves into a fighting frenzy once more. Meanwhile, reports had come in that the southern colonists were gathered at Isleta Pueblo, and so it was decided that all the people of the kingdom would come together there. We left our smoke-blackened homes on the twenty-first, the armed men marching with ready weapons all around us women, old people, and children. Some oxcarts carried food supplies, and in one of them were the sacred vessels and holy images from the destroyed parish church of the Immaculate Conception. They were later turned over to the care of my Confraternity and inventoried in its books.

One of the household images that escaped, though "wounded," was that little copy of the Toledo Virgin which had foretold the Indian rebellion and the ruin of the kingdom. A friar eventually took it down to the city of Mexico, where it was long after venerated as Our Lady of La Macana, because it had been damaged by an Indian war club.

I myself left Santa Fe clasped in the arms of a young housewife, who pressed her wet and trembling cheek to mine and wept as she trudged along with the rest. Her name was

Josefa López Sambrano de Grijalva. She was the wife of Francisco Lucero de Godoy, son of Francisca Gómez Robledo, and eldest grandson of Francisco Gómez and Ana Robledo. Now I was retracing, in reverse, the journey I had made with Father Benavides in 1625. At Santo Domingo Pueblo, headquarters of the Franciscan Mission Custody, where Father Benavides had stopped while I went on to Santa Fe, we found the bodies of three slain Fathers and of five other Spaniards. All along the way the enemy tried to ambush us, but fled when our men went out to fight them. Further south we found the despoiled corpses of men and women, and learned more details of other massacres from Indians captured along the way. We also discovered, even before reaching Isleta Pueblo, that the southern colonists had fled all the way to El Paso del Norte, since they had been told by the Indians that every single soul in Santa Fe and the northern haciendas had perished. Governor Otermin then decided that we all might as well go down to that distant and southernmost mission.

This is how I once again saw the now deserted mission of the Assumption at Socorro, made the hot and dreary Jornada del Muerto once more, saw again the unchanging face of Mount Robledo, and slipped with the wild north river through the defile among sugar-loaf stone bluffs into the valley of the old river ford, El Paso del Norte. But where nothing had been in 1625, there now stood a fine mission surrounded by many houses.

## CHAPTER VI

T HE Mission of Our Lady of Guadalupe at El Paso del Norte was fairly new. Although at this spot Oñate had taken formal possession of New Mexico in 1598 before proceeding northward with the colony, and the place was often traversed afterward by the wagon trains and other parties traveling to and fro between Santa Fe and the city of Mexico, no one had lived there permanently until a Father of the Custody founded this southernmost of the New Mexico missions in 1659 under the title and patronage of Our Lady of Guadalupe. Around it he gathered the roving Suma Indians. After some eight years of trouble and temporary abandonment of the project, the large adobe mission with its beautiful carved ceiling beams was blessed on the fifteenth of January, the year 1668. Into this twelve-year-old home of Our Lady of Guadalupe my exiled and fugitive people brought me at the end of that sad August in 1680.

It was the first of the New Mexico missions named for the Maiden of Tepeyac, strange to say, and I will dwell on this fact later on when speaking of the origin of Our Lady of Remedies.

Governor Otermin settled his homeless subjects at fertile spots on either bank of the Rio del Norte down from the mission. The Spanish folks set up their own villages, while the southern Tigua and Piros Indians, who had fled with the colonists of the southern district, founded their own pueblos.

These towns were rearranged later on.

San Lorenzo, named for St. Lawrence because the friars were martyred on his feast, was the seat of the exiled government of New Mexico, the Santa Fe of the south. For the first three years it stood many miles down the river, but in 1684 it was moved up closer to the mission. Here my people built a small church and dedicated it in Mary's honor under my popular title of Our Lady of the Conquest. This was to be my home and throne until the day we returned to Santa Fe.

Those thirteen years of exile could have been happy ones, for the land was good, the winters mild, and the King had aided the impoverished settlers with food, clothing, and new implements. But as with every large group of people, there were some, and not the neediest, who took the lion's share of his Majesty's aid. Then the wild Texas Indians, upon learning that the pueblos of the north had bested and driven out the invincible Spaniard, thought that they might as well finish the task by killing the fugitives or driving them further south. Their attacks on the new villages were fierce and frequent. But what mostly broke the spirit of the New Mexicans was their failure to reconquer the kingdom. Three successive governors tried, rather halfheartedly, and failed. Family after family began petitioning the viceroy for permission to settle further south in what is now the Chihuahua country. Others ran away from the colony. A new kind of leader was needed to restore the pride of my people.

Yet I must say that their attentions to me did not waver in the least, as may be seen from the gifts I received during the period of exile. Of the dresses and ornaments donated before the Rebellion, only a few remained, and they were in very poor shape. My crowns were lost. Still, there were over thirty pieces of jewelry in 1686, three pairs of earrings among them. I also had seven chemises with ruffs of various colors, and two plain ones; five dresses and four skirts of different colors, made of silk or gold lamé, and edged with gold braid; also six hoods of various fine materials. Of my mantles, there were three blue ones, one with gold and silver flowerwork, and the others with gold scallops; also a green one with gold scallops, five plain white ones, and a Seville mantilla of black lace.

Between the years 1687 and 1693, I acquired a silver crown and two new dresses, one of white French figured silk, and a red one of Chinese figured silk, all from Francisco Lucero de Godoy, nephew of Francisco Gómez Robledo and husband of the woman who carried me out of Santa Fe in her arms. A friar inspector of the missions had my hoods and chemises destroyed, also a hat with plumes, because he said that the Holy Office had forbidden certain items of dress on sacred images.

During this time of exile there was one very sad occurrence, for me. In 1684, Francisco Gómez Robledo relinquished the presidency of my Confraternity to another man, after so many years of devoted service. He was too sickly now to carry on this labor of love, much less go on those futile Indian campaigns. If my eyes had been real the day he signed over the Confraternity books to his successor, they would have poured hot tears down my cheeks. But he came to see me often in my church at San Lorenzo, until he could no more.

Then a new knight appeared, in the person of a new kind of governor of the kingdom.

## CHAPTER VII

DON DIEGO de Vargas Zapata Luján Ponce de León had a lineage in Madrid that was much longer than his name. However, he was too genuinely noble to fall back on his ancestry for support. His not too tall, delicate-looking frame; his, oh so suave and handsome face; his sweet low voice — all belied the fact that in armor he became a giant whose spoken commands brought squadrons to valiant attention. If I describe him like a woman captivated by a man's graces, it is because he, too, fell in love with me soon after his arrival at Guadalupe del Paso in the year 1691. Or, rather, he was so piously and gentlemanly devoted to the Mother of God in heaven that he loved any image of her that he met, especially if it was beautiful like myself and had a history. And my own people were not slow in telling him what I had meant to them and to their own forefathers all these years.

Nor was I jealous, of course, when Don Diego de Vargas showed his admiration for the royal standard of the kingdom of New Mexico, which had the royal arms of León and Castile embroidered on one side, and the image of Our Lady of Remedies on the other. It was an old banner which, the people told him, had led Oñate's army in 1598 for the founding of the colony, as also in many a colorful campaign and ceremony in the years that followed. With this standard unfurled before him and his revived forces of New Mexico militiamen, our new governor and captain-general set out to reconquer the kingdom at the close of summer in the following year, 1692.

First went the supply carts and pack mules, the artillery

and other such units, to wait at Mount Robledo, where the entire expedition was to assemble. Then, on the twenty-first of August, the royal standard was unfurled in the plaza of Guadalupe del Paso, and Don Diego with his main forces set out for the north. The cheering, praying crowds saw visions of the days of Cortés, or of Oñate's men in 1598 chopping down the yelling hordes of savages on the sky city of Acoma. Some of the soldiers feared that they might never return to their wives and children, but most of them harbored dreams of distinguishing themselves in combat as had their grandparents and great-grandparents ninety-four years before, something for their own grandchildren to boast about in years to come.

But as the army entered the first inhabited pueblo and then another, and another, both officers and men began to marvel at the tactics of this new captain-general and the impact of his personality on the Indians. Although at first ready to fight without giving quarter, these Indians were won over by his voice and presence. Then, dismounting, Don Diego embraced their chieftains. Next, displaying Our Lady of Remedies on the royal standard, he told them in his simple and sincere manner how both Indian and Spaniard could now live in peace together under so tender a Mother who loved them all alike. And it worked!

When they reached Santa Fe, where the Indians outnumbered them ten to one, the rank and file of soldiers were at first tense with misgivings, but it worked here too. On Sunday, the fourteenth of September, which was the feast of the Exaltation of the Holy Cross, they marched into Santa Fe with all possible martial splendor, after the initial parleying was over. Around a great cross erected in the ancient plaza, the Padres sang the *Te Deum,* and the natives joined with the Spaniards in shouting their joyful allegiance. So it went in all the pueblos, even the populous and fierce centers at Jémez, Zuñi, and the faraway Moqui pueblos on giant cliffs against the sky. Always, it was the fatherly word, the brotherly gesture, the motherly image floating over them in the breeze.

Within four months, twenty-three pueblos of ten Indian nations had been conquered without the loss of a single life, Spanish or Pueblo Indian. What was more touching, many women and young folk who had been believed slain in 1680 were found in captivity and taken back to their relatives. On Saturday, the twentieth of December, the victors reached Guadalupe del Paso, and Don Diego de Vargas went "into the holy temple, the church of Our Lady of Guadalupe, to give thanks to her blessed Majesty." Then he wrote a long report to the viceroy, telling how he had embarked under the protection of the "Sovereign Queen, Most Blessed Mary, Our Lady of Remedies," and through her had achieved a bloodless conquest.

On receipt of the wonderful news, the city of Mexico and other centers of New Spain went wild with the ringing of bells, Masses of thanksgiving, and popular fiestas. A fly sheet relating the whole venture in poetic prose was printed, and copies were sown abroad, so that in all Spain and her New World colonies Don Diego de Vargas had become the most talked-of hero of the times.

Here I find it most proper to relate the story of Our Lady of Remedies, which I have promised all along.

It is recorded that in the year 1540, nine years after the apparition of Our Lady of Guadalupe on Tepeyac to the Aztec Indian Juan Diego, and also to his uncle Juan Bernardino, there lived another Indian on the western side of the Valley of Mexico, and he was a cacique or village chieftain. His town stood at the base of a large hill called Totoltepec, and the man's Spanish name was Juan de Tobar.

One day, while hunting on top of the hill near his home, Juan found a very small wooden statue of Mary, about a hand high, holding her Child on her left arm and a scepter in her right hand. It lay almost completely hidden among some rocks underneath a maguey or century plant. Juan took the statue home and made a little altar for it, and there it stood for almost fifteen years. It turned out that this tiny image had belonged to a soldier of Cortés' army who hid it when fleeing from the great massacre of June thirtieth, 1520, *"la noche triste"* when the Aztec warriors of Mexico cut the Spanish forces to pieces. Many people, mostly Spanish folk, were flocking in such increasing numbers to venerate it that Juan de Tobar finally took it to the village church from his house. This was in the year 1555.

Not long after, this Indian chieftain fell grievously ill. Crippled and blind, he had some of his subjects carry him to the flourishing shrine of Our Lady of Guadalupe by Tepeyac at the north end of the valley. As he neared the holy painting, Juan suddenly found himself completely cured. What his healed eyes saw first was Our Lady's portrait, and she was saying to him with motherly reproach: "Why do you come to my house, after you have put me out of yours?" Then the Virgin told him to return home and see to it that a chapel was erected for the little statue he had found, and on the very spot where he had found it. He gladly obeyed, and ever after the chapel and its statue, and the hill on which the shrine stood, were known as Our Lady of Remedies.

This is the beautiful story. However, what follows is very silly, since people can often act foolishly when blinded by some passion; and a passion blinder even than that of the flesh, it seems, is that of race. After relating the apparitions of Our Lady of Guadalupe, which brought about the mass conversion of the southern Indians of New Spain, I remarked that the Spaniards as a whole did not take too kindly to the miracle. Those born in Europe were the most reluctant, while those born in America were more inclined to favor the Indians. As I began to say, in spite of all the evidence before them, these Spaniards fought Our Lady of Guadalupe with their minds, ignoring the promptings of their hearts which they dared not admit to each other. Why, they thought, should holy Mary, who has had her champions for centuries in the Spanish captain and caballero, why should she give her portrait to these low Indians steeped in idolatry?

To overshadow the fame and popularity of Our Lady of Guadalupe, they adopted this little Lady of Remedies as their own patroness, since it had come from Spain in heroic times and had belonged to a Spanish conquistador. (Their passion overlooked the fact that an Indian had had everything to do with its discovery and original fame.) Great pompous processions were conducted frequently, in which the Spanish grandees of the city of Mexico bore Our Lady of Remedies with viceregal pageantry from her shrine to the cathedral. At last the viceroy himself, in 1574, and the city Council, removed the shrine of Remedios from the care of the Franciscans at Juan de Tobar's village, and placed it under the Government's direct patronage. A sumptuous church supplanted the first chapel, and Our Lady of Remedies came to be known as *La Gachupína,* the European-Spaniard, while the holy painting of Guadalupe was referred to as *La Criolla,* the Creole.

Such childishness was enough to make the Savior and His Mother weep and laugh at the same time, were it not that they understood human frailties so well.

All this also explains why there was no mission titled Guadalupe in the kingdom of New Mexico until the one at El Paso del Norte was founded many years after.

But Don Diego de Vargas, for all his faults, stood far above the great conquistadores of the past. Mary, to him, was the tender Mother of man's Divine Savior, enjoying the company of her Son in heaven, from where she regarded all men as her own children for having been redeemed with the

Blood of her Son. Therefore, no matter what her image, or whatever its name and title, no matter to whom given or by whom venerated, it was also his to cherish with all his heart.

As we have seen, he used Our Lady of Remedies, as pictured on the royal standard, as the means of pacifying the Indians in his recent glorious campaign, for the success of which he went before a copy of Our Lady of Guadalupe to give thanks. Now it was my turn. Now that my people were preparing to return home to New Mexico and Santa Fe, he would walk alone of evenings to the rosary and novena devotions in my little church at San Lorenzo. On January the sixteenth, 1693, he wrote with deep feeling to the viceroy:

"It is my wish, with those with whom I enter, including the soldiers, that they should, first and foremost, personally build the church and holy temple, setting up in it before all else the patroness of the said kingdom and villa, who is the one that was saved from the fury of the savages, her title being Our Lady of the Conquest."

## CHAPTER VIII

ONCE again, sixty-eight years after my first journey to Santa Fe with Father Benavides and Francisco Gómez, I was riding north over the very same route, and enclosed in a wagon. Well ahead, some parties far in advance, rode the components of De Vargas' Army of the Reconquest. Since the triumphant entry of last year it had grown in numbers with the addition of many officers and soldiers who had been recruited in Spain.

But now my two-wheeled wagon was not merely one of many freight carts wearily advancing in a lonely single file. I was surrounded by laughing women and their children of every age. The youngest, born at Guadalupe del Paso during the thirteen-year exile, were viewing the land of their fathers for the first time. Older ones remembered landmarks as we went along. Adults recalled people they had known, found dead and despoiled in 1680.

Some pretty young women walking nearby argued about this or that mountain or rock that we passed, but most of the time they talked about the new young soldiers from Spain. Each had already picked out her man, whether he knew it or not. It did my heart good, or the wood grain within me, to hear their joyful voices, for among them were the daughters of Andrés Gómez Robledo, who had died in the defense of Santa Fe thirteen years before, when they were little girls. They were my dear dead Francisco's nieces, granddaughters of Ana Robledo, and the last to bear the family name, for there was no man of the family left to return home with me. One girl,

Margarita, was already married to a dashing young captain from Asturias, and another, Francisca, was betrothed to a nice young private from Compostela.

The triumphant entry into Santa Fe on December 16, 1693, I will never forget. Upon our arrival, the governor had settled us women and non-fighting folk at a low spot against the hills a little to the northwest of the town, where we were more protected from the cold north wind. His troops made their camps on the heights, from where they could keep an eye on the Indian-occupied capital and on our camp below, as well as the entire countryside for miles in every direction.

Now, about eleven o'clock in the morning of the sixteenth, our people and the Tanos Indians filled the plaza in front of the Palace of the Governors and even the flat rooftops all around. In through the gates came the governor's Negro herald, a war drum hanging at his side and a bugle in his hand; after blowing a fanfare, he announced the arrival of the royal standard, and then began to rattle his drum with magic sticks. Riding a lively charger, the royal ensign for the occasion, Don Fernando Durán y Chávez, appeared with Our Lady of Remedies displayed aloft on its tall staff. The crowds broke out in cheers for Our Lady and the King. Then came the ranks of the infantry, followed by the cavalry, all falling into parade formation before the palace's lengthy front. And last came Don Diego de Vargas himself, accompanied by all the military and civil officials, and the Fathers of St. Francis. Room had to be made for them by mounted captains who pushed the crowds back from a tall wooden cross in the center of the plaza. And the cheers kept on rising and floating off to the snow-topped mountains.

De Vargas solemnly turned the missions over to the Fathers, and the city to its mayor and Council. Next he spoke kindly to the Indians, pardoning every one, and promising all the

Pueblos peace and good treatment from now on. The settlers then went to their camp outside, to give the Indians time and freedom to gather their belongings and return to their former homes in the Galisteo Valley. However, a few of the colonists did stay inside the town. I had forgotten to say that Santa Fe now had a tall sturdy wall of adobe all around, which the Indians had built while we were away. Large sections of that wall held the adobes of the old parish church, whose foundations alone remained.

The Tanos Indians did not leave as expected. They found excuses for delaying their departure, and De Vargas readily accepted them, although our people were complaining about living out in the open in the bitter cold. The Padres hounded the governor for not having a church for the divine offices, and so, on the eighteenth, De Vargas went over to examine the chapel of San Miguel across the river. Its thick walls still stood intact; only the roof, burned off in the siege of 1680, was missing. Summoning the chieftains together, he asked them to repair the roof of the chapel. Such a task ought to be a most cheerful one, he told them, to make a house for the Lord, and also for me, who was still enclosed in a wagon without home or throne; for if a lady should visit any of them, would they not feel themselves in duty bound to furnish her with a house? Ah, the knightly thinking of a nobleman from Old Madrid! But the Tanos Indians knew nothing about chivalry toward ladies, and the plea fell on deaf ears. But they were shrewd enough to take hold of the governor's own remark about the cold weather, and told him how beams and lumber could not be gotten now because of it. And De Vargas excused them generously once more. They found new excuses for not vacating the town, and again he was patient, day after day.

The weather grew bitterly cold. The Lord's Nativity found the colonists in the open camp suffering terribly as the snow flurries swept down from the sierra in thick white curtains. Husbands and fathers remonstrated with Don Diego; they felt that the Indians had planned some kind of treachery. Then, those individuals who had stayed inside the walled town came out with the news that the Indians had decided to fight to retain Santa Fe, and soon the Tanos were taunting the Spaniards from their barricaded positions, calling out in broken Spanish how neither God nor Santa Maria could save them now from perishing of cold and hunger. It was the twenty-eighth of December.

Early next morning my people took me off the cart and set me up on an improvised altar in our camp. The companies of soldiers, headed by their captains and lieutenants, aligned themselves in martial formation before it. Still looking very much disturbed and disappointed, Don Diego De Vargas knelt at the head of them all while everyone recited the act of contrition in a loud voice. One of the Fathers imparted the absolution, followed by a brief talk. Then, as the royal standard was handed up to the mounted royal ensign, and the order for assault was given, the rest of my people began praying the rosary amid tears and lamentations.

All morning long the repeated Spanish attacks proved futile, on account of the high walls and the moat. At noon a wave of screaming Tewas from the northern pueblos rushed down the hill slopes to attack our soldiers from the rear, but a quick turn-about charge by the cavalry routed them completely and with great slaughter. Night fell, and still Santa Fe was in Indian hands. If they were to be dislodged, a strategy of surprise was needed, something the Indian feared — surprise and darkness.

Caught off their guard well before daybreak, the Tanos' defenses fell apart in one swoop. The clash of steel and the battle cry of "Santiago" in the darkness completely unnerved them, so that dawn found the banner of Our Lady of Remedies on the highest roof of the Palace of the Governors. Seventy captured warriors with their leaders were executed in the plaza that morning; hundreds of others had fled before sunrise, leaving their women and children at the mercy of the victors. These De Vargas turned over grimly to the colonists.

This was the first time that the great calm governor had lost his kind composure with the Pueblo Indians. Nor could he be blamed too severely, after having been so tolerant even when his own subjects suffered so much because of his patient forbearance. The Indians' perfidy had most of all wounded his pride, and deeply, for his world-famous peaceful campaign of the previous year had been brought to naught in a single day. Afterward he relented and had the defeated Tanos with their women and children settled in a new pueblo near Santa Cruz. But even here the Tanos showed their undying hate, for three years later they incited the northern Pueblos to murder their missionaries and many of their Spanish neighbors.

The rest of the Pueblos, in general, continued giving De Vargas trouble during his first term as governor. They had defeated the Spaniard in 1680 and discovered his feet of clay; they thought it could be done again. The heathen tribes, like the Apaches, also made many raids to capture horses, which they prized very much. All this made one campaign after another necessary, and so the parish church and my promised throne were still unbuilt.

In the year 1695, I am proud to say, De Vargas persuaded the members of my Confraternity to elect him *mayordomo,* the first governor of the kingdom to hold this office. He also gave me several costly gifts, in lieu of the church and throne he was not able to build as yet, not only because of Indian troubles, but also hindrances from his own people. His successor as governor, Don Pedro Cubero, who had bought the office from the King, arrived to take over in July of 1697, and he immediately threw De Vargas into prison under charges of malfeasance in office. To erase from memory whatever good De Vargas had done, or so it seems, Cubero even assumed the presidency of my Confraternity; he gave me an imperial gold-plated crown inlaid with stones, together with a red brocade dress and a mantle of blue brocade — as if to outdo a blue dress of figured silk and a white mantle that De Vargas had donated. He further ingratiated himself with the Fathers of Santa Fe by building them a large friary.

But my champion, after his release from jail, had returned to the city of Mexico, and there so completely cleared himself of Cubero's false charges that he was made a marquis. Eager to keep his promises to me, he asked to be reappointed as our governor, and by the time he reached Santa Fe, Cubero had slipped away by a different route.

Don Diego arrived in November, 1703, but by the following spring he was dead. Taken seriously ill in the Sandia Mountains while pursuing Apaches who had stolen all the settlers' stock at Bernalillo, he was carried down to that village and there breathed his last in early April of the year 1704. In his last will, made on his deathbed, he commended his soul to his beloved Lady of Remedies. Later, among his effects, there were found many small images of Mary, and of various titles, and among them a precious one of Our Lady of Remedies.

Once again death had robbed me of another plumed knight, while I, of brittle and dead wood, lived on because of her whom I represent. I still did not have my own palace and throne. Following the battle for Santa Fe, I stayed in a tiny chapel inside a tower of the Palace of the Governors, where the governor and his aides worshiped. Some time later I was placed in a temporary parish church, dedicated in honor of St. Francis, which De Vargas had built behind the palace, by the north city wall.

Before passing on to the next century, I wish to relate that there were many weddings after the battle of Santa Fe. And I must name that of Francisca Gómez Robledo to young Ignacio de Roybal y Torrado, the new soldier who had come from a little village near the great shrine of St. James the Apostle in Compostela.

I must also make note of the fact that many new families came from New Spain to join the old colonists. De Vargas had requested them from the viceroy for the Reconquest, but they arrived many months after. But from that particular wedding, and from among these new settlers, were to come those who did the most to keep my memory alive until this day.

Toward the end of the century I had eleven complete changes in my wardrobe, counting the two dresses and mantles from Governors De Vargas and Cubero.

## CHAPTER IX

THE new century began with a sad note, not only on account of De Vargas' death in its fourth year, but mainly because of the hardships my people were undergoing in establishing themselves once more in their homeland. The unrest among the Pueblos had died out by 1700, but the depredations by wild nomadic Indian tribes fell like a scourge from the four winds. In spite of all this, my people did not waver in cherishing me, even though they were prevented time and again from rebuilding my parish church. I was called in as a mute witness by persons reclaiming ancestral lands. The ignorant swore by me in petty matters, although this was the wrong thing to do. The expeditions that went out against the wild Indians were always placed under my protection. Thus Governor Cuervo thanked me publicly, in a letter to the viceroy, for the success of a major campaign in 1706; and again in 1719, acting Governor Valverde did the same after routing the Utes and Comanches.

This is not to say that there were no light, or even comical, occurrences. In 1712, for example, someone who had a grudge against the Padres wrote his complaints in a letter which he placed in my hands, sure that the Fathers would find it there. The ensuing furore was enough to make a wooden statue smile.

My chief knight at this period was Don Juan Páez Hurtado, one of the officers from Spain recruited by De Vargas. First as a personal aide, and later as his lieutenant general and governor, he owed everything to Don Diego and was grateful. He had taken an active part in the famous peaceful entry of

1692, when he also received an Apache arrow in his leg as the army was returning in triumph to Guadalupe del Paso. He missed, however, the second entry of 1693, and the battle of Santa Fe, as he was down in New Spain gathering the new colonists. This is why, when he inaugurated the Santa Fe fiesta in 1712 to perpetuate the memory of De Vargas, he chose to commemorate the first bloodless expedition in which he himself had participated, and vividly remembered from the arrow wound.

To De Vargas, also, he owed his love and devotion toward me. Having been appointed the executor of his master's will as well as interim governor, Páez Hurtado also took over the presidency of my Confraternity, on the first of May, 1704. I am sure the ladies would like to read the inventory of my wardrobe which he himself wrote and signed on that day. It was as follows:

"First of all, a new dress of silk with gold flowers, embellished with a fine French galloon matching the flowers of the silk fabric, with a mantle of gold-flowered blue silk with the same embellishments; another dress of gold-flowered blue Florentine silk, much worn out, and without mantle; another dress of Florentine silk with red, green, and blue flowers, worn out, and without a mantle; another dress of white lamé, old, with a mantle of white gold-flowered silk embellished with an imitation gold galloon a finger wide; another dress of brown silk with white flowers, adorned with imitation buttons which serve as a border, old, and without mantle; another white dress of old tapestry embellished with gold-point lace, without mantle; another dress of green tapestry without ornament and mantle, much worn out; another dress of blue camlet with an old blue embroidered mantle; a gilt silver crown with twenty-five imitation stones, green, blue, and red, with its surmounting cross; another old crown of plain silver."

That Juan Páez Hurtado promoted my glory for the rest of

his days is shown by the fact that he was buried under my altar on the fifth of May in the year 1742. His second wife had been laid to rest close by within the sanctuary of my chapel six years before.

These burials remind me to relate how the parish church and my throne had meanwhile come into being. In the year 1714, ten years after Governor De Vargas died without being able to fulfill his promise, the large parish church was begun on the east side of the plaza, almost on the same place where Father Alonso de Benavides had built his church after my arrival, and where the Apache chieftains came to admire me in my role of the Assumption. This new building was much larger, and was now dedicated in honor of good St. Francis, whose little chapel of the Assumption at Assisi, better known as Our Lady of the Angels, is famous the world over as the Portiuncula.

My Confraternity of the Rosary was largely instrumental in bringing the building to completion. Also, connecting with its north transept, the members built me a large chapel with intricately carved beams and corbels, like those they had seen in the mission of Guadalupe del Paso. Here at last I had my throne. It would have delighted the great heart of De Vargas. But to come back to those burials. It was the custom in those colonial days to bury people in the earthen floor of new chapels and churches until all the spaces were filled. The most influential people, like governors and mayors and captains, together with their families, got the places of honor, those closest to the altar. That is how Juan Páez Hurtado and his wife found their last resting place so close to my throne. The rest of my promoters and admirers all wanted to be buried in my chapel, but by 1743 there was no more room left.

This is the very chapel in which I dwell today. During the last century, when Santa Fe was made a diocese, then an archdiocese, her first bishop and archbishop built a fine Romanesque cathedral of stone around the old adobe parish church, which was then pulled down in 1884, and the debris hauled out the new building's front door. The new north-side nave had cut through the forward, or entrance, part of my chapel, but the rest of it was spared. Later an arched opening was made between it and the new cathedral, so that the ancient adobe chapel of La Conquistadora, though so very poor and primitive in appearance and materials, is now the Lady Chapel, and richest part by far, of the historic cathedral of Santa Fe.

Don Bernardino de Sena was my next devoted herald. This man, dead now for two centuries, means nothing to you or anyone else; for that matter, neither do Juan Páez Hurtado or the Gómez Robledos, or many other persons too numerous to record here. But to me these particular people were the salt of the earth. Were it not for them I would not be known; perhaps I would not even exist today with a story to tell.

Unlike his predecessors, Bernardino had a poor start in a poor land. He had been born in the Valley of Mexico, not far from the shrine of Guadalupe, and as an orphan had been adopted by a childless couple who came to Santa Fe in 1694. The boy was some nine years of age at the time. Through honest labor and an exemplary life, he gained both prestige and property in the capital, where he married a very good woman who gave him one son, Tomás Antonio, in their twenty years of married life. After her death he married a daughter of Francisca Gómez Robledo and the soldier she had wed after the battle of Santa Fe. This second wife had no children in their twenty-nine years of marriage, but they did rear several orphans.

Bernardino was *mayordomo* of my Confraternity for almost half a century, from the year 1717, when the parish church was completed, until his death in 1765. Though the governors ceased to be elected presidents of my Confraternity, it does not mean that they neglected me; there was Don Antonio de Valverde attributing a victory to me in 1719; and some years later Don Domingo de Bustamante gave me some very fine dresses and a mantle. However, as Bernardino grew older and older, membership in my society dwindled more and more. Was it because the same man was re-elected, or because the governors no longer were chosen presidents of it? Perhaps for both these reasons. But the real cause lay in the fast-growing poverty of the people, the common folk who had been the chief supporters after all, and their failing spirits. And these were directly caused by the depredations of the Plains Indians which were worse than ever before. And so my Confraternity languished into extinction as the year 1760 approached, the year when a new and lively Confraternity of Mary suddenly burst into being.

In this year of 1760, the affluent Governor Francisco Marín del Valle completed a large chapel on the south side of the Santa Fe plaza, directly across from the Palace of the Governors. It was to serve both his staff and the *presidio,* or garrison, hence was also known afterward as the *Castrense,* or Military Chapel. In fact, it was the very first military chapel in New Mexico. There had been a small chapel in the ground floor of a tower of the Palace of the Governors before 1680, and it was reopened for use by De Vargas in the year 1693; it was always known as a hermitage of Our Lady because the royal standard was kept there. However, this tiny oratory was not big enough to admit more than a squad of soldiers. Here the governor's chaplain, who was also chaplain for the garrison, said Mass for the governor, and his family and aides, on regular Sundays. On big occasions everyone went to the parish church, where the governor had his canopied chair in one of the transepts.

Now, at last, the garrison had a chapel that rivaled and in many ways outdid the old parish. What made the Castrense so different from any other church in the whole kingdom was the altar with its great reredos and pulpit — all carved out of white stone. This stone had been hauled all the way from a hill at Los Ranchos de Pojoaque, and the intricate carving had been done by craftsmen from the city of Mexico whom Governor del Valle had brought up for this purpose. In the open center panel of the great reredos, and canopied with curtains as though enthroned, was a large bright painting of Our Lady of Light. It depicted Blessed Mary with her Child snatching a youth away from the jaws of Satan. The same picture was done in white stone and imbedded high on the exterior front wall of the chapel. People from all over the kingdom came to see this marvel of the century, and to learn about Our Lady of Light.

The original painting was made in the seventeenth century for a great Jesuit preacher in Sicily, Father Antonio Genovesi, who used it with great success in his mission preaching. It was brought to the city of Mexico in the year 1707, and in 1732 was donated to the city of León in New Spain; there, in 1767, it was solemnly enshrined in the principal church of León which later became a cathedral. This was the special devotion of Governor del Valle and his wife, and they did their utmost to propagate it during their short stay in New Mexico.

With the ceremonies of dedication in 1760, the Confraternity of Our Lady of Light was launched under the auspices of the governor himself and of the Bishop of Durango, who was in Santa Fe at the time. He was the first bishop to visit the kingdom in thirty years. With a bishop inaugurating the society at the time he blessed the imposing chapel with pontifical splendor never seen before by most of the citizens, the Confraternity had a wonderful beginning; with this chapel and its marvelous reredos as its headquarters, it far outshone my own humble society that had been. All civil and military officials joined it. The leading men and women of the capital lent both their names and their resources to its furtherance.

Yet I myself was not forgotten. Far from it. I was still visited daily, even by those who had pledged their adherence to the new society. For in their hearts I was still very much their ancient Queen.

This Confraternity of Our Lady of Light died out a few years after the governor's term was up and he returned home. I was sorry to see it dwindle away so fast, for it had come like a burst of sunlight after a stormy night. Though a female, and an actress besides, I could not for a moment decry something that had brought more glory to Mary as well as new spiritual life to my people. Thus I had rejoiced at the triumphs of Our Lady of Remedies on the royal standard, and the devotion that De Vargas had toward her. I was happy over the ever-growing popularity of Our Lady of Guadalupe since my people had lived in exile near her mission for thirteen years; now you could not find a home without a little painting of her, or at least a cheap print; and two northern Indian missions now bore the title of Guadalupe, a new one at Pojoaque Pueblo, and that of Halona Pueblo in Zuñi, which had been refounded in 1706.

But sometimes I wonder if the devotion of Our Lady of Light had depended too much, perhaps, on loud fanfare and pomp, on the power and affluence of the great.

## CHAPTER X

THE year 1776 is a most significant one for all America, and even the rest of the world, but most especially for this our northern continent. Far to the west of the kingdom of New Mexico, on the great ocean's edge, the first missions of California were being established by Fray Junipero Serra, a Franciscan with the energy and foresight of my Fray Alonso de Benavides, but with much more of the inner fire of their Father St. Francis. He had already founded his first mission of San Diego in 1769, and that of Our Lady of Sorrows at San Francisco was being born in this very year of 1776.

And far away on the eastern coast of North America a new nation was also being born. My own people knew nothing about it. Although they had heard of English colonies thousands of miles east of the vast bison plains and a great river, they had given them no thought, content that they stayed there. Not even the echo of a New England shot heard around the world reached Santa Fe on her mountain perch. Little did my people know that this new nation would grow by leaps and bounds and, within seventy-five years, would engulf their old kingdom on its fast course westward to Father Serra's newborn missions on the Pacific shore.

It was in this same year of 1776, significantly, that a Franciscan priest was sent up to New Mexico with orders to inspect the missions and report on them thoroughly, and also to find a good route from Santa Fe to the newly opened territory of California. In doing so, Father Domínguez described me and my chapel, and also my wardrobe, although he did not approve of my Confraternity, because there were no documents to show that it was lawfully founded; whereas that of Our Lady of Light had excellent papers with the seal of the Bishop of Durango. Of course, no papers existed for mine, as they had been destroyed long ago, in 1680. And this my Confraternity was not exactly the ancient one which all my champions had fostered until Bernardino de Sena's time. It was, rather, a refounding of it, a real rebirth, and this is how it happened.

Only let me say that for this particular year of 1776, my *mayordomo* was none other than Bernardino's son, Tomás Antonio de Sena, a real and living continuity, to say the least.

Seven years previously, in 1769, Captain Don Nicolás Ortiz, a leading citizen of Santa Fe, who was lieutenant governor at the time, was killed in battle with the Comanches near Abiquiu. His body was brought to Santa Fe and interred with great mourning in September of that year. When Governor Mendinueta went to console his widow, Doña Josefa de Bustamante, she made an urgent proposal regarding myself. By the way, this lady belonged to the family of that governor who had given me some precious clothing some thirty-five years before; she was also a prominent charter member of Our Lady of Light. She proposed to Governor Mendinueta that I should be solemnly chosen as Queen of New Mexico, and that a Confraternity ought to be founded under my patronage, to beg God's mercy on the kingdom, for the roving pagan Indians had become more menacing of late.

It was the same old Spanish custom of turning specifically to Our Lady of the Rosary when the enemy was at the gates.

At this latter part of the century, you see, the Plains Indians had grown in numbers considerably, for the Eastern tribes that the English did not exterminate had fled west of the great river to the middle prairie country. They now had swift horses, bred from animals stolen or strayed from the Spanish settlements of New Mexico, and they rode them better than the white man. The French traders of the Mississippi Valley were selling them firearms in exchange for hides, buckskins, and pelts of every kind. So now these Indians were outmatching the fighting men of New Mexico in every way, raiding the river settlements all the year round. People now risked their lives by merely working in their own fields along the Río del Norte.

Mendinueta agreed to the proposal, and the Fathers of Santa Fe were ready to help. The governor himself ordered a most beautiful dress made for me in the city of Mexico, and also a fine carved chest with lock and key in which to keep it. Once again I was the exclusive center of attraction among my people. But it made my heart weep to see that these dear folk, although they had never forgotten me, did not remember my devotees before the Rebellion of 1680, like Francisco Gómez and Ana Robledo. They no longer knew of Josefa López Sambrano who had carried me out in her arms on that sad August day. All they recalled now, and vaguely, was that I had come to Santa Fe with the great Don Diego de Vargas and, consequently, supposed that it was he who had brought me here for the first time. Because he had peacefully and without bloodshed reconquered the kingdom in 1692 with the banner of Our Lady, they thought that I in some manner had taken an active part in a battle free from bloodshed.

Soon after, the people began taking me out in procession from my old chapel at the parish church to the place outside the city where the colonists had encamped before moving into Santa Fe. There, under a *ramada,* or shrine of boughs, I was enthroned for nine days, and a Mass was chanted every day during the novena. Then another procession brought me back home to the parish church until the following year. This was something new. Of course, I had always been taken out in procession, and several times during the year, on my feast of the Holy Rosary and other major feasts of Mary — before the Rebellion, during our exile at Guadalupe del Paso, and back here in Santa Fe ever since the days of De Vargas. What my people were observing now were the novena processions held in the city of Mexico and Puebla for their own ancient Conquistadoras, whose stories I have already told. The custom fitted me perfectly, I must say, as the Conquistadora of my very own kingdom, and it pleased me very, very much.

I said these novena processions were new, that is, compared with my already long reign in New Mexico and Santa Fe. But let it be remembered that at this time the oldest California missions were just being founded, while the new nation of the Thirteen Colonies on the Atlantic coast was just being born.

Before going on, I must tell about my transformation and my wardrobe in 1776. First of all, Father Domínguez described me briefly but sharply by noting that I was about a yard tall, very old (of course), and recently retouched. He somehow insulted me, although I hardly blame him, for my face had lost much of its original beauty, not so much from age as from inexpert treatment at the hands of my loving people. They sometimes washed my plaster face with strong soaps, and then tried to repair the damage with hands that knew nothing about sculpture or painting. And this Padre from the city of Mexico, used to seeing the last word in art, was rather cruel in his veracity. Had he known my full history, he would have written quite differently, I am sure.

"She has many ornaments," said he. "But since she is always getting a complete change of clothing, her current dress is not described now, save that she always wears a wig." That wig! In recent years the wearing of wigs had become the fashion. It was a French custom which Spain and England and their American colonies avidly copied. As I, too, was a lady, some kind soul believed that I would look much better and more in style with real hair. And so my carved auburn locks above my brow were fearfully hacked away, leaving an ugly cut above my hairline; the sides of my neck were also badly scraped. No wonder that I now wore a wig "always." And it was not a creation from Versailles like that of Marie Antoinette, or even those worn by the viceroy in the city of Mexico, or the signers of the Declaration of Independence in New England, but a stringy homemade affair.

My wardrobe, however, was much better. Besides underclothing of cambric and Brittany fabrics given to me by Governor Mendinueta, and some tiny undershirts for the Infant sometimes placed in my arms, there were these outer garments: A dress and mantle of plain white satin with gold braid, a dress and mantle of silver and blue material embroidered with gold, and five other pairs of dresses and mantles in various colors. There were also matching dresses for the tiny Infant, a little black felt hat for myself, an extra wig with the hair made wavy or fuzzy, a gold-plated silver crown and another of plain silver, and dozens of jewelry pieces, like earrings, necklaces, and so forth. Oh, yes; my right hand held a small military officer's baton at this time.

## CHAPTER XI

T HE "Secular Period" is the name sometimes aptly given to the closing years of the eighteenth century in New Mexico, and the first half of the nineteenth, up to 1850 or so. This is because the Bishop of Durango had "secularized" the parishes of Santa Fe and other main towns by assigning secular or diocesan priests to take the place of the Franciscan Fathers. By this time, anyway, the Franciscans had become fewer and fewer, because of a serious falling off at their chief headquarters in the city of Mexico. So that when the priests sent from Durango refused to stay and returned home, the state of the Church in New Mexico continued in its rapid decline. The aging friars who hung on, and a handful of native clergy ordained by the bishop, were not enough to stem the tide.

The old Indian missions in the pueblos began to fall down, and the abandoned Indians gradually turned back to what they remembered of the old heathen gods, although holding on to external practices and customs of the Church. The Spanish folk, too, especially in the remote villages, began to lay more stress on outward observances than on essential matters, sometimes falling into superstition. For this is the bane of religion anywhere without proper guidance. Yet they clung heroically to the faith of their brave forefathers, always remembering it as a divine legacy brought first to Spain by the Apostle St. James, and from there to the New World and up to their own isolated kingdom that once had been through the apostolic ministry of the sons of St. Francis. Away from the capital, my memory faded almost completely among the impoverished and abandoned descendants of my former courtiers and minstrels. In my stead, and in the place of other images that had disappeared, they cherished their *santos*.

I must explain these so-called *santos,* since often I am mistaken for one of them. Please, not that.

What are now properly known as New Mexico *santos* are the very crude images of the Savior and of His saints which the native people made during this Secular Period. In the beginning, as when Father Benavides brought me to Santa Fe, and also after the De Vargas Reconquest, the Spanish Crown had furnished fine statues and paintings, from the best art shops in Spain and New Spain, to every single mission in New Mexico. The colonists had also brought little household images of the same quality. But time had destroyed or disfigured most of these, and there was no one who could restore or replace them. New statues and paintings, with the rare example of the chapel of Our Lady of Light and its treasures, had ceased coming, just as new priests and friars failed to come and replace the old.

The result was that this or that Padre, deeming himself an artist of sorts, made some statues that were positively ugly, so much so that Father Domínguez, already in 1776, condemned them as unfit for stirring up devotion. But still, these were not what is now meant by *santos,* for even in their hideousness there was an attempt to reproduce the human likenesses accomplished by real sculptors.

During the Secular Period, some utterly untaught native craftsmen, in order to supply new churches and chapels and many homes with greatly needed and wanted images, began to produce something entirely new. Almost wholly unhampered by traditional modes of art, and pouring out their simple peasant devotion through their unguided hands, they brought forth images that portrayed more the idea that was represented than any actual human resemblance. For example, a crucifix showed less correctly the bodily features of Christ Crucified, and more the sufferings that He underwent for man's sin. In short, they portrayed Suffering itself.

The images painted on flat pieces of board are all most charming. But only a very few of the statues are true works of art; they even foreshadow by more than a century the style of art that is called modern. The vast majority, however, though well meant, and having admirably served their purpose in their day, are monstrosities unfit to represent holy Mary and the saints, much less our Divine Redeemer, whether in homes or in the churches. The bishops of Durango rightly condemned them, as did the first bishop of Santa Fe and his clergy regard them with strong disfavor.

Now that the collecting of them has become a fad, almost like that of collecting old shaving mugs, and the word *santo* has become an arty byword for old sacred images, many are prone to class me among them. Please, I am not one of them. Though spoiled by the passing of centuries, and also by deliberate mutilation and worse repair, I am still a statue of Mary that was fashioned by a real sculptor, and once upon a time I was as beautiful and perfect as any statue can possibly be.

The people who lived in Santa Fe, where I still reigned day and night as their Queen, did not lose sight of me for a moment. Perhaps because I was the only palpable object left from the dim and faultily remembered past, they clung to me as though with loving desperation. The great governors and captains had departed, and the written records of the conquistadores had been lost. Only a little wooden Queen remained who had represented their heavenly Mother and Queen to their own forebears in what to them seemed ages ago. My yearly novenas and processions went on with undiminished vigor and gathered added significance as the past, glowing like a Golden Age in folks' fancies, grew cloudier in its actual details within their memories.

This is how, in the year 1806, I got another chapel, which is today known as the Rosario. The builder of it was a wealthy old gentleman by the name of Antonio José Ortiz, who had recently rebuilt not only the sanctuary of the old chapel of San Miguel but also the entire nave of the parish church that had fallen down. Significantly, he was the grandson of Juan Páez Hurtado, that old knight of mine whose bones lay beneath my altar. His wife, Doña Rosa Bustamante, was the younger sister of that fine lady, Doña Josefa Bustamante, who had given new life to my Confraternity in the days of Governor Mendinueta.

To replace the temporary shelter of cottonwood and juniper branches, so far erected annually for my novena, Ortiz made this Rosario chapel for me. Both he and the lingering old friar-chaplain of the Santa Fe garrison knew, when the chapel was built, that this was the spot where I had waited with my people as De Vargas and his forces fought for the city of Santa Fe. Alas, however, for peoples' memories. The next generation was saying that here had stood a former chapel built by De Vargas himself in compliance with his vow. And the following generation went on to claim that this very chapel, built by Ortiz in 1806, was the very one erected by De Vargas more than a hundred years before. To me it was all very amusing, God bless them all. For they lost sight of my chapel at the parish church, which was really the oldest; and they dated me with De Vargas, when I had been their forefathers' Queen a century before that.

I am sure that you would like to take a look at my wardrobe shortly before my Rosario chapel was built outside the city, also at myself. By 1796 I had been forced into a niche covered with glass on four sides. I say forced, for to fit me into it a carpenter sawed off my pedestal, right through the clouds at my feet and the chins of the cherubs. And to make the door close, he shaved off the tip of my slightly bent right knee.

My dresses with their mantles were five in number, and different from those described twenty years before. One was of gold and yellowed-silver cloth, and bordered with brilliant silver lace, and the blue mantle was also covered with silver gauze — all tinsel, as you can see. The others were not much better, but still in the old queenly style: a dress of white brocade with gold edging, and its mantle of the same color lined with pearl-hued ribbed silk; another dress and matching mantle of pearl-colored satin, all lined with silver flowers; a cheaper one with unlined mantle, both made of satin of various colors and trimmed with Dutch lace; and the fifth a dress without mantle made of silver lace and gauze on a pearl-hued background. These were the last royal dresses and mantles that made me look like a Spanish Queen of olden times, for, after they fell apart one by one, I began to be attired in a different fashion, as you will see later on. Yes, I began to look almost like one of those *santos* from the hills.

While my people of New Mexico, no longer a kingdom but a poor forgotten frontier province, dreamed on in their isolated mountain villages, or their green oases along the desert-bordered Río del Norte, great changes were· shaking the outer world. It is true that my New Mexicans had to contend with enemies much too close at hand, the Apaches and Comanches, the Utes and Navajos. But they knew nothing of vastly greater battles between giant nations elsewhere, of how ancient monarchs were toppling from their thrones, or at least losing large parts of their kingdoms. The English colonists had set a pattern in 1776 which was beginning to disturb other colonial centers in America that were in contact with the outside world.

In 1810, New Spain, the fabulous empire of the Aztecs and then of the viceroys, the land favored by Our Lady of Guadalupe as Mary has favored no other nation, rebelled against the Spanish monarchy. With a great shout the priest Hidalgo raised aloft the image of Guadalupe on a new banner that, ten years later, led the mixed people of his country to form a new nation, called Mexico after the ancient city conquered by Cortés and built into Roman and Parisian splendor by the viceroys. However, Hidalgo's shout was but faintly heard among us; it was almost as inaudible here as the shot at Lexington that made the world look up. Everything was so far away, up on the moon, almost. My people became aware of a change in government merely by the change of flags on the Palace of the Governors.

In less than twenty-five years my tired people were to change their allegiance again, and just as passively, to that new nation of 1776 which had grown into a young giant and was approaching ever closer across the bison plains.

But whatever the type of government at the palace and garrison, I was still Queen at the parish church. Vicars from the new Republic of Mexico, who came to inspect the dilapidated missions and make reports to the Bishop of Durango, took but fleeting notice of me and so mentioned me briefly, in passing, as of little consequence. I meant nothing to them, naturally, and their great cathedrals and churches of intricately carved stone down south had statues and images that were far more imposing than I. What is more, Mexico had Our Lady of Guadalupe, whom my own people also loved dearly, compared with whom I am but an insignificant piece of willow carved by human hands.

However, I cannot leave unmentioned what one Mexican

governor did for me. Don Mariano Martínez de Lejanza, the last of four governors who came to us from the Mexican Republic, planned to have a beautiful shaded park around my Rosario Chapel, as well as a wide tree-lined avenue for my annual processions from the city to the park and chapel. The trees were planted at Rosario, and a special ditch was built to lead water to them from the mountains, before he was recalled home.

Nor will I ever forget good Bishop Zubiría, the last prelate of Durango to rule the Church in New Mexico, who, in his final pastoral visitation in 1850, warmly renewed his approval of my chapel at Rosario and the annual processions in my honor.

## CHAPTER XII

THE times were changing fast indeed. But of the many changing things in this ever-changing world, there is none so sure, and so often unpredictable, as the change of styles in dress. To men it is not overly important, but to the ladies, even to a wooden lady, the problem is paramount. If I appear to be getting philosophical on this question, it is because — well, I must say it — I came to wear a Mother Hubbard, of all things.

For more than two hundred years, from the day my carved golden arabesque robes of a Semitic Princess had been spoiled by a cruel knife, I had worn the graceful regal tunics and mantles of a medieval Spanish Queen, even when my people followed the trends of the times.

Military dress had changed considerably, from the morions and breastplates of Oñate and Francisco Gómez, through the flatter helmets and corselets of De Vargas' times, to the armorless knee breeches with long-tailed coats and tricornered hats of Mendinueta's period; then, from the early nineteenth century long trousers with tailed ball-buttoned shortcoats and small sailor hats, followed by tall shakos and Napoleonic cockades of the Mexican Revolution, down to the plain blue uniforms of General Kearny's American Army of the West, which in the summer of 1846 marched into Santa Fe and raised the Stars and Stripes over the Palace of the Governors.

The dress gowns of women kept pace with the style set by European courts, though in New Mexico the new modes could be afforded by a meager few — the current governor's wife and the wives of some of the leading captains. But the daily dress of all the women, the rich as well as the poor, had varied little during these hundreds of years. Both young and old wore what is now called the peasant blouse, but with long sleeves, and the long and ample, and ever graceful, peasant skirt. The variety that women perennially seek was effected by the quality and color of the material, as well as laces and other trimmings in the form of ruffles. A small triangular shawl of various colors and designs covered the shoulders when going out; a lace veil on the head, with or without comb, when attending church. Old women and those in mourning covered themselves with big black shawls that made them look like nuns; and since old age came early in those hard times, and so many members of each family were being killed in Indian raids or campaigns, this black attire came to be the most common one.

However, no one thought of trying these styles on me, neither the festive style of the moment worn on state occasions by the leading ladies, nor the everyday dress of everyone. As their Queen, I always wore what in Spanish lands had become the traditional dress of Mary, the royal robe and mantle from the days of Isabella. These are the ones I have described at different periods.

But after the coming of the American Army, there began to arrive fair-haired ladies who wore different clothing, and covered wagons drew up at the plaza with new goods and fabrics to be displayed and sold in stores. The Sunday dress of these new ladies was usually very charming, consisting of a high tight bodice and ample skirts with or without ruffles and bustles; the long tight sleeves had what they called mutton-leg shoulders, and often the high lace neckpiece cascaded down the bosom in delicate lace creations. Needless to say, our women copied these styles and looked very well in them, and I myself would not have been unwilling to try them in those times.

Our New Mexico women also adopted the daily dress of

the American newcomers. But this was not pretty at all. They gave up their old Spanish peasant dress, which was taken up and later developed further by the squaws of the now-tamed Navajo Indians, and put on plain calicos of one piece, unadorned, often without anything to give the dress character at the waist, save for a work apron. As my regal dresses and mantles of 1796 had fallen apart, they began to dress me in these plain shapeless ranch dresses. Oh, indeed, they were mostly of silk and even garnished with laces and bows, but they lacked shape; and since my mutilated upper half and my puppet arms lacked grace, I could not contribute my share by filling them out properly. Yes, I did begin to look like those *santos* of the last fifty years. My old crowns had disappeared, and now I went out on my annual processions dressed like a tasteless ranch wife, sometimes with a little tin crown on my head, or even a wreath of paper flowers (or those wax orange-blossom sprigs worn at weddings), my coarse hair streaming in stringy strands to the wind.

My beloved people, though, still thought me most beautiful. Their hearts were the same, and I was content.

Soon after the arrival of the American soldiers and the appointment of the first American territorial governor, Santa Fe became a diocese, exactly two hundred and twenty years after my Father Alonso de Benavides had made the first suggestion, and in 1851 Bishop Lamy arrived to take over the old adobe parish church and my chapel as his cathedral. He was a Frenchman, and the priests he brought were countrymen of his who gradually began to fill all the old Franciscan parishes and missions, and to establish new ones. The bishop, who afterward became an archbishop, built his great cathedral of stone, as I have already related, around the old church, which was then demolished. But my own throne room was spared and was later joined to the new cathedral to form its north chapel.

The French rectors of the cathedral, and their assistants, took to me with reservations at first. I do not blame them. How could these men, in whose country the fashion for female styles has been set for so long, find any attractiveness in my appearance? What is more, I was unknown outside of Santa Fe, and they had Our Lady of Lourdes, who was famous the world over. Mary Immaculate had appeared to Bernadette and turned a spot in southern France into a fountain of miracles and a perennial song in Mary's praise. This Lady of Lourdes was now introduced to my people in the form of beautiful colored prints and delicately finished statues that were crowned with flowers during the month of May.

But the continued faithfulness of my people in Santa Fe in carrying out my yearly processions and novenas, their daily visits to me at the cathedral, and my old history as related by them from their faulty memories, brought these French gentlemen to regard me with deep respect. However, they themselves added to the existing confusion regarding my true name and identity. In translating the word "Conquistadora," as a Lady who had conquered or gained a victory, they began to refer to me as Our Lady of Victory, in Spanish as well as in English. They were also led to this mistake by their acquaintance with a famous shrine and image of Mary in Paris, Notre Dame des Victoires. But she is Our Lady of Victory, not I.

All this happened less than a hundred years ago. Since then the times have further changed, faster and faster. New governors and new captains have come and gone, new archbishops and new priests. New wars have touched my ancient kingdom in one way or another, among them two great conflicts that drenched the entire world with blood and took the sons of my people to faraway shores where many of them now sleep.

Old Father Alonso de Benavides, all the Gómez Robledos, Don Diego de Vargas, Doña Josefa Bustamante, and all those noble souls whom I remember as though it were yesterday, would not recognize their kingdom of New Mexico and their villa of Santa Fe if they came back today, except for the everlasting mountains and the blue of our sky that is like none other.

And they would recognize me, their Queen. I am still here, as always.

## EPILOGUE

IF EVER *you should come to Santa Fe, you will find me in my same old Conquistadora Chapel in the Cathedral of St. Francis of Assisi. It is not a sumptuous shrine, but the venerable adobe walls and the carved brown ceiling are napped with soft rich memories. The dust beneath the flooring is all that remains of many who centuries ago paid me living tribute and in death keep me faithful company. From the living you will find tokens of humble remembrance, like a burning candle or a bunch of home-grown flowers, the quiet presence of an aged woman or a young man praying. If there are bouquets of more costly blooms about, you can be sure that some happy bride left me the flowers from her wedding that morning.*

*You will now find me dressed in the attire of an ancient Spanish Queen, as in the days of Ana Robledo and Diego de Vargas, though what the color of my mantle may be at the moment I cannot say, for I have several. The favorite one is of a pale blue brocade, made from what was left of a two-hundred-year-old cope, and the dress that best goes with it is one of white and silver figured silk embroidered with minute roses, and bordered with a brilliant gold braid that never tarnishes, though centuries old; this dress once belonged to an image of the Virgin in Guatemala. Or I may be wearing a reddish mantle of Chinese figured silk edged with bright silver lace; this is one of my old mantles that survived; it was done over again and strengthened with a new sturdy lining. Not so good are two white dresses and a white mantle, with embroidered flowers and crosses, which were made from pieces of old French vestments; the material does not wear its age well. My newest and costliest dress and mantle are of cloth-of-gold brocade, with golden cords and tassels on the back and a family crest embroidered in front; they were made for me last year in the German city of Speyer.*

*Also changeable without notice are the Sevillian lace mantilla that covers my hair and is held in place by a crown, and the earrings showing beneath it among my dark locks. Or I might have my little Infant Jesus on my left arm, which is fastened to my mantle, or both my hands might be empty save for a rosary of gold colored beads.*

*My imperial crown is of stamped brass, but handsome, with imitation stones. This is for everyday wear. A precious one of filigree is now being made for me.*

*My expression, you will note, is somewhat sad. Almost all Spanish Madonnas are sad. But my wistful look is also the result of so much damage and poor repair down the centuries. Several years ago a fine sympathetic artist of Santa Fe was asked to restore my features, but he merely repaired the parts that were crumbling and repainted my face exactly as it appeared at the time; for he rightly felt that I ought not to look according to his own fancy, but as the years and my people had brought me to look. And I myself might as well reflect in my expression the many sorrows that my people have bravely undergone these many long centuries, and also appear as though I am always thinking of my loving knights and courtiers who are no more.*

*But at the same time I manage to keep the triumphant air of that Lady conceived without sin being borne aloft into eternal glory. Neither age nor mishandling have erased the dignity and poise that belong to a Conquistadora, a Lady who has conquered.*

*Beneath my feet may also be seen a small gold-painted pedestal, which replaces the one sawn off and lost long ago. Though it is covered with antique rococo*

# THE AUTOBIOGRAPHY OF AN ANCIENT STATUE

*molding to go with my ancient self and the style of my garments, it is really a modern work of precision underneath; it is an eight-sided block of white pine that was cut and fitted together, and purposely, in the humming shops of the atomic city of Los Alamos, not long after the first bombs went off at Alamogordo, then at Hiroshima and Nagasaki. For, as I myself am, allegorically speaking, a prayer to her who crushed the infernal serpent's head, so this pedestal under my feet represents a continual prayer that Mary may hold vanquished underfoot whatever there may be of evil in atomic power.*

*Every year now, on a late Sunday afternoon in June, as my procession winds slowly down the narrow streets of Santa Fe to my chapel at Rosario, I can make out the atomic city against the blue mountain flank, a thin white blur that turns into a necklace of lights as darkness falls. And the soft Spanish syllables of the Ave Maria go up to heaven pleading in a haunting old Spanish melody: "Santa Maria . . . ruega por nosotros pecadores . . ."*

*Borne high on the slender shoulders of white-veiled girls, I see in my bearers, and in the thousands of persons forming my entourage, the same people who took me out year after year these three centuries and a quarter. Like their forefathers, they bear uninterrupted witness to my glory, and I bear witness to their ancestry. And now, besides them, there are other people here, new faces that increase with every year. They are those who revered the Mother of God in other places, and whose forebears rendered her homage in other lands. Having come to live in this my land and love it as their home, they also love its Queen. They, too, are mine and dear to me.*

*For this reason, and because my old kingdom is a sister state of all the other United States of North America, whose faithful Catholic subjects long ago placed themselves under the mantle of Mary Immaculate, I would love to visit their great skyscraping cities*

91

*someday, and go into their precious churches, from
the coast of the Atlantic all the way across this vast
continent to the Pacific shore. Now that men can travel
overland in as many days as it took oxcarts months,
now that they can outfly the eagle and even the eagle's
own scream, this wishful dream could well come true.*

\* \* \*

*Yes, it is a far cry, too, from that olden day when
a willow tree yearned in vain to wear the meadow's
dress of flowers, not knowing that one small part of
it would outdo old Solomon in all his glory, and even
the very lilies of the field, by playing the part of her
who is the Rose of Sharon and the Flower of Carmel.
And like a coat of many colors I have also worn the
adventurous joys and burdens of my loving people
these three hundred years and more, close to the verge
of destruction or oblivion more than once, but now
more colorful and beloved than ever before.*

*Of course, I know that I myself am not immortal.
The day will come when I shall join the rest of the
willow by being burned to ashes, if not in fires set off
by man, most certainly in that day when all the stars
will fall. Nevertheless, I shall live on in the memories
of those my courtiers who see God face to face, and
behold His Mother's real beauty forever, for having
fulfilled her prophecy in the Gospel by calling her
blessed in every generation until the end of time.*

# POSTSCRIPT: 1974

Talking about destruction or oblivion, I almost went the way of all flesh and wood last year when I was kidnapped. Yes, actually kidnapped! A pair of youths took me from my throne one night, expecting to sell me through a fence the way old "santos" have been stolen these days and disposed of for a good price. But the poor lads had not reckoned with my uniqueness, much less with the excitement caused among citizens of all faiths when I was found missing. For, since the year this autobiography came out, more people had come to realize so much the more how much I meant to the colorful lore of their homeland. In the meantime, I had been honored with episcopal and papal coronations, along with gifts of new crowns and wardrobes and even a diamond cross. My two chapels had been wondrously renovated, and even new streets were named after me. And, now I will confess to some vanity, I was making headlines in the national press.

The main fear among all and sundry was that the thieves might destroy me in their panic, even after they decided to hold me for ransom and folks began raising the large sum demanded. I must admit that I felt that this was the end as I lay bundled inside a dark old mineshaft in the Manzano mountains south of Albuquerque. But, to make this postscript short, I was finally restored in triumph to my ancient throne, even though I had to spend some time in the Santa Fe jail as criminal evidence. For one of the dear rascals had broken down and confessed, leading my rescuers to the site of my durance vile.

---

# POSTSCRIPT: 1984

*The 1980s.* This decade began with the third centenary of the Pueblo Revolt of 1680. That was when my people and I had to leave our beloved Kingdom for a 13-year exile far away. These days, as their very descendants continue observing my annual processions, which recall our triumphant return with the so-called DeVargas Reconquest of 1693, some newcomers to our land harbor a kind of wonderment. How, they ask, can my pretty role as a Conquering Lady be reconciled with conquests and reconquests that speak of blood and carnage?

The answer is simple, as I have tried to show from the beginning. My peculiar Spanish title has nothing to do with battles as such, much less with bloody assaults of human beings upon one another. What La Conquistadora means is that I came with the first settlers who called themselves *conquistadores,* and who from the start took my little wooden self as a symbol of the heavenly as they saw it. And so the historic events that I witnessed, both in 1680 and 1693, are being remembered as periods of survival and reconciliation.

Those were sad times indeed, those days of war-clubs and muskets. But they have been followed down to this very day by much deadlier arms on land and sea and air, in wars around the world in which my Kingdom's brave sons of every race and belief have also died. But what witnesses will survive, including my wooden self (as if that mattered), when, as I just hinted a short while back in referring to grim forces discovered at nearby Los Alamos, an infinitely more horrible weapon is let loose upon poor mankind? Heaven forbid!

## *BIBLIOGRAPHY & HISTORICAL COMMENT*

The documentary evidence and references for this true story can be found in my historical study, *Our Lady of the Conquest* (Santa Fe: 1948), which is an expansion of an earlier article, "Nuestra Señora del Rosario La Conquistadora," in *New Mexico Historical Review,* Vol. XXIII. The theory first proposed here, that the statue is the one of the Assumption brought by Benavides, is brought to further certainty in a later article, "La Conquistadora Is a Paisana," in *El Palacio,* Museum of New Mexico, Vol. 57. Other manuscript references not contained in the above works may be found in my book *Origins of New Mexico Families in the Seventeenth and Eighteenth Centuries.* Here, too, will be found the scores of individuals who kept the devotion alive.

All facts on Our Lady of Guadalupe of Mexico are taken from a compendious work in two tomes, *Historia de la Virgen de Guadalupe,* by an anonymous Jesuit (Mexico: 1897). Here also may be found the origin of Our Lady of Remedies of the city of Mexico.

Data on Our Lady of Guadalupe of Extremadura in Spain are from a booklet, *Real Monasterio de Guadalupe* (Vitoria: 1951), by the Franciscans of that shrine, and from my conversations with them.

The story of La Conquistadora of Puebla comes from Fray Agustin de Vetancurt's *Crónica de la Provincia del Santo Evangélio.* The prophetic incident concerning the image of Our Lady of the Blessed Sacrament of

## LA CONQUISTADORA

Toledo is in his *Teatro Mesicano,* Part IV, Tome III. Its fate and subsequent title of La Macana may be found in "Barreiro's Ojeada," *New Mexico Historical Review,* Vol. III, and in Canon Garcia Gutierrez' Ramillete de Flores Marianas (Mexico: 1946). Here also is found the origin of the painting and devotion of Our Lady of Light.  Fr. A.C., O.F.M.

Bacigalupa, Andrea. *Santos and Saints' Days.* Santa Fe, NM: Sunstone Press, 1972.

Cary, Diana, and Ortega, Pedro Ribera. "The Conquering Lady." *St. Joseph Magazine,* Vol 59, No. 1, Jan. 1958, pp. 3-5.

Chavez, Fray Angelico. "La Conquistadora - Her 350th Anniversary." *New Mexico Magazine,* Vol. 53, No. 9, Sept. 1975, p. 30.

—————————. "La Conquistadora Is A Paisana." *El Palacio,* Vol. 57, No. 10, Oct. 1950., pp. 299-307.

—————————. "The Conquistadora Processions." *New Mexico Magazine,* Vol. 55, No. 6, June 1977, pp. 33, 47.

—————————. "Nuestra Senora del Rosario La Conquistadora." *New Mexico Historical Review,* Vol. 23, Nos. 2 & 3, April & July, 1948, pp. 94-128 & 177-216.

—————————. *Our Lady of the Conquest.* Santa Fe, NM: Historical Society of New Mexico, 1948.

Espinosa, J. Manuel. "The Virgin of the Reconquest of New Mexico." *Mid-America,* Vol. 7, No. 2, 1936, pp. 79-87.

Espinosa, Jose E. *Saints in the Valleys; Christian Sacred Images in the History, Life and Folk Art of Spanish New Mexico.* Albuquerque: University of New Mexico Press, 1960.

Ortega, Pedro Ribera. *La Conquistadora: America's Oldest Madonna.* Santa Fe, NM: Sunstone Press, 1975.

—————————. —————————. New, Bilingual Edition. Santa Fe, NM: Sunstone Press, 1983.

Patterson, Robert M. *The First Lady of Santa Fe, La Conquistadora.* A Broadsheet, Vol. 1, No. 1, 1954.

*Provincial Chronicle.* "La Conquistadora Lost and Found." Vol. 40, No. 2, Oct. 1973, pp. 39-41.

Randolph, Courtney. "La Conquistadora." *Westways,* Vol. 40, No. 6, June 1948, pp. 2-4.

Rogers, Vern. "The Lady of the Conquest." *New Mexico Magazine,* Vol. 39, No. 8, Aug. 1961, pp. 29-30.

*Santa Fean.* "La Conquistadora." Vol. 3, No. 1, Dec. 1974-Jan. 1975, pp. 29-32.

Woods, Will. "A centenary for Mary." *St. Anthony Messenger,* Jan. 1954, pp. 6-8, 61.